to Robert Norfleet

with congratulations on May 1975

John Brown

EVERY
MOMENT
AN
EASTER

EVERY
MOMENT
AN
EASTER

CLIFF R. JOHNSON

PREFACE

THOUGH THERE OUGHT TO BE a more original way to say this, I must call attention to the crucial fact that a sermon prepared to be *heard* and a sermon prepared to be *read* are two widely different means of communication. I shall make no effort to support this thesis; it is really widely enough recognized to need no argument or demonstration.

This homiletical fact of life does mean that many ministers who feel that with God's help they do manage to offer a few fragments of the bread of life from the pulpit on Sunday morning are hesitant to put these same sermons into print. The hesitancy grows from the realization on the part of the minister that people who heard the sermon and felt some uplift at the time may be keenly disappointed upon *reading* the sermon at a later time.

This difference between a preached sermon and a printed sermon is likely to be at its greatest for a minister who has an informal conversational style of preaching. If my analysis has any accuracy, then this is the manner of my own preaching.

Ernest McIver, Jr., and I are trying an experiment with this book of sermons. Here is a series which I preached on the Apostles' Creed. A number of folk were kind enough to insist that they would like copies. I had them taped as I preached them, and then had them transcribed, just as they were delivered. Now, Ernie McIver has edited them as little as possible, hoping thereby to retain the informality of their original presentation.

We have had these sermons set up in a format which also aims at conveying something of the emphases of the verbal presentation. Whether the device is successful, the reader must decide.

I have deliberately, and distinctly, aimed this effort at the members of Westminster Church, whom I know and whom I love and *who heard the sermons preached*. It is really for them, alone, that I have much hope that this book may prove rewarding.

If others, who did not hear the sermons, find themselves enriched by any measure at all from reading them, then so much the better.

It was Ray Torpy who was principally responsible for the taping, Dorothy Smith and Edith Frazer who did the transcribing, and McIver Art and Publications, Inc., which provided the book and jacket design.

A couple of friends who would be embarrassed if I mentioned their names advanced the money to pay for the private printing until the sale of the book could provide for at least partial repayment.

C.R.J.

Alexandria, Virginia
December, 1962

CONTENTS

THE APOSTLES' CREED

I believe in God the Father Almighty, Maker of heaven and earth; and in Jesus Christ His only Son our Lord; who was conceived by the Holy Ghost; born of the Virgin Mary; suffered under Pontius Pilate; was crucified, dead, and buried; the third day He rose again from the dead; He ascended into heaven; and sitteth on the right hand of God the Father Almighty; from thence He shall come to judge the quick and the dead. I believe in the Holy Ghost; the holy catholic church; the communion of saints; the forgiveness of sins; the resurrection of the body; and the life everlasting. Amen.

GOD,
THE FATHER
ALMIGHTY

S EVEN YEARS AGO on this very Sunday I began a series of sermons on the Apostles' Creed.

I don't know that its being seven years ago is particularly important—except that number seven sounds sort of scriptural and significant—but anyway it *was* seven years ago,
> and in that we recite the Creed every Sunday morning,
> and in that there are a lot of changes in this congregation in seven years,
> and in that I can at least hope that my own thinking and feeling have undergone some change,

I feel it's time to preach such a series again.

So, between now and Easter, we shall work through the Creed—with a Sunday off here and there for something else that may come up in the church's program.

We shall move forward in no compulsive fashion, and these sermons—whereas they shall all be on the Creed—are not to be so related as to make it difficult for you to follow if you should miss a Sunday now and then.

The Apostles' Creed is one of the three oldest creeds of Christendom,

creeds to which the church has given the name *ecumenical*—
that means used by the whole church
Protestant
Roman Catholic
and Eastern Orthodox.

I think there's a little significance in the particular Sunday on which we begin talking about the Creed that is shared by us and our Roman Catholic brethren—sort of a coincidence. I wish that I could say that I foresaw this, and this came out of my wisdom and planning
but it didn't
so I might as well be honest.

I picked up recently a little piece of literature which I hold in my hand—there are some copies out in the vestibule—gotten up by several Protestant ministers in town and at least one Roman Catholic priest. It's a prayer for a week, starting Wednesday, for the unity of the Church.

To me it's a great piece of literature because it's the first time I've seen anything gotten up by the Protestants and the Roman Catholics together in which there is no undertone of contention, or of guarding one's position, or of any implications of secondary positions for one or for the other.

Unless I'm very much mistaken, the Roman Catholic priest who is participating in this is the young priest, Father Quinlan, up here at Blessed Sacrament. I think he is one of the outstanding young priests in the Washington area and bids to go far in his service of God and in his service of his church.

He's starting this series of lectures on Wednesday night—to which the Protestants are invited—and then, mirabile dictu, as he himself would say, he and some of his parishioners are going to be at the First Christian Church the following week one evening for a social evening.

I could be cynical about this and could say that I could be more strongly committed to this effort at unity if the Vatican Daily Observer—or whatever the name of it is—wouldn't come out just exactly at the same time with a comment from the top echelon saying that —leave us not be deceived—the faithful might as well

10

recognize that any unity of the Church will come as other people come back to Rome.

But let that be as it will. Let's accept this as it is on its face as a sincere and tremendous overtone . . . something started here in Alexandria that might go a long, long way. Anyhow, it's good for me, and I shall be praying for the unity of the church, because with my contentious spirit in this area, it's very much in order that from time to time, my own spirit should find that which will challenge it and discipline it . . . and maybe, by the Grace of God, soften it a bit here and there.

But back to the Apostles' Creed.

The tradition that it was put together by the apostles is, of course, pure fiction. The story which arose—I think probably in the fifth or sixth cenutry—is that each one of the apostles contributed a sentence and then the whole thing, having been thus knit together, was given to the church. Of course, there is no ground for that at all . . . it's pure fiction. But it *is* true that the Creed—the Apostles' Creed—is very old, going back perhaps to the Roman Christians of even the second century, in a somewhat abbreviated form.

I'd like to read this oldest form which we have in the Greek from the year 335 A.D. The implication there is that it is already very old. If you like, look in the back of your hymnal, on page 53, for the Apostles' Creed, or I think there are some cards there in the pews that have the Apostles' Creed on the back of them . . . one place or the other so that you may follow. I shall try to read slowly so that you see how the Creed was being said in the year 335 A.D. and how surprisingly close it is to the Creed as you have it there in your hands.

"I believe in God the Father Almighty and in Jesus Christ, His only Son, our Lord, who was born of the Holy Ghost by the Virgin Mary, was crucified under Pontius Pilate and was buried. The third day he arose from the dead. He ascended into Heaven and sitteth on the right hand of the Father. From thence He shall come to judge the quick and the dead. And in the Holy Ghost, the Holy Church, the forgiveness of sins, the resurrection of the body, Amen."

The other phrases which we now use were added here and there by various localities in Europe over the course of the next 300 years. So the Creed as we have it now exactly did not take its full form until perhaps the seventh century. But you see, the whole great core—really the essence of the Creed—is there back to the second century.

The other two creeds grew out of early theological controversies—the Nicene Creed was put together, I believe, in 325 A.D. This creed and the next one I shall mention, together with the Apostles' Creed, are Presbyterian creeds.

Our Episcopal brethren use the Nicene Creed more than we do—we use it rather rarely. They have it in their prayer book and it has a beautiful liturgical ring, for it's the Nicene Creed that has "God of God, Light of Light, Very God of Very God," and so forth and so on. It's our creed, too.

Then some several centuries later we have the other ecumenical creed used by Protestants, Roman Catholics, and Eastern Orthodox, called the Athanasian Creed. There's not very much we know about its formulation except that it was not formulated by Athanasius. Nevertheless, here are these other two creeds—the Nicene and the Athanasian. If you compare them with the Apostles' Creed you will see them to be just basically commentaries on this old, old creed.

From time to time I sway back and forth in my commitment to the Creed and to its use. At the moment, I'm rather strongly for our using it because it does bespeak the deepest unity of the church universal. As I said a bit earlier, I particularly need that for my own recurrently contentious spirit. But more to the point, I think that it *should* and *can* mean something specifically for you. We can recognize, as we are doing now, that every phrase —indeed almost every word of the Apostles' Creed—has to be reinterpreted if it is to have meaning for the twentieth century.

So be it. We're trying to do it now.

It can serve as a peg on which to hang your theological convictions, so that if someone comes up to you and says, "You're a Presbyterian, what do you believe?" you can stop this thing of fumbling and stumbling around and going on the defensive and getting all confused about what you *do* and *don't* believe, and ending up with some poor-grade argument on predestination.

The next time somebody asks you what you believe as a Presbyterian, start out by saying, "I believe in God the Father Almighty, maker of heaven and earth, and in Jesus Christ, His only son, our Lord, who was conceived by the Holy Ghost . . ." and so forth and so on, down to the end.

All right. When you do that, you will be using the Creed for its original purpose, for the Creed grew out of the instructions of the catechumens in the earliest days of the church when it seems that the teaching of the Creed was always verbal—it was never written down. There was something esoteric, sort of secret, about it. Perhaps because there were the pagan religions that also had their secret rites, and the Christians felt like they didn't want to be left out of the running. Perhaps, also, they feared that the Creed might be misused.

We do know that this was taught by word of mouth as the last instruction that the catechumen received after he had finished everything else. So then the first time that he said the Creed publicly was when he was baptized, and thereafter it became sort of his spiritual union card, if you please.

I believe in God the Father Almighty, maker of heaven and earth.

This magnificent phrase needs to be looked at as a whole, for this opening phrase is not designed to put you on the side of people who believe in God. Rather, it's to put you on record as to what you believe concerning God's essential nature. Not whether God exists, but the *kind* of God you believe in:

I believe in God the Father Almighty, maker of heaven and earth.

I myself, and speaking for myself, am committed to the conviction that the existence of God—the very existence of God—is what philosophers call a *first truth*. And that is that we are immediately aware of the fact that there *is* God just by virtue of the fact that we are human. Other first truths, comparably, are beauty, and goodness, and truth itself . . . and time, and distance.

13

You see, the characteristic of a first truth is that you can deny it and when it is denied, there is no way to prove it. Your opponent has only to deny it to defeat you.

Take, for example, beauty.

You are speaking to someone and you say, "the world is full of beautiful things—this is beautiful, and that is beautiful, and that is beautiful," and he needs only to say, "there is no such thing as beauty," and you cannot possibly even prove the existence of beauty.

Or truth.

What are you going to use to prove the existence of truth?

Or goodness.

These are things of which we are immediately aware. And I believe that we are immediately aware of God as existing.

What of the atheistic communists?

For myself, I think it's quite possible that as we see now, the commies have their hands full in trying to make their atheism stand up within their own framework of their own people. For myself, it could be that this very fallacy might be the thing that contributes most directly to communism's ultimate downfall.

Be that as it may.

I remember reading somewhere, a long time ago, that that magnificent woman who has challenged us all, Helen Keller—deaf and blind—when she finally broke through to humanity by virtue of being able to speak with her fingers on someone's hand, said to someone who was talking with her, "I have always known God—I just didn't know His name."

This matter of the existence of God is a place where we and our Roman Catholic brethren do have a somewhat different approach.

They speak of *proofs* of God's existence.

We say, "No. Call them arguments for His existence, or evidences, if you please, but not proofs, for we can neither prove nor disprove the existence of God."

14

I'm not sure whether this difference in the approach of Protestants and Roman Catholics in their theology makes much difference—maybe it does, maybe it doesn't. But for your information—and perhaps passing interest—there have been four classical arguments—or proofs, if you wish—for the existence of God. They have nice long impressive names, and when I was in seminary I had to learn each one of them and know how to speak about it and speak of its weaknesses and of its strengths.

Here are the names . . .
   the cosmological
      the teleological
         the anthropological
            and the ontological.

Now, doesn't that sound learned? If I only knew what they meant! No, I do know what they mean.

Let me impress you further.

I'll say this very briefly because I don't expect you to carry it in your mind. The cosmological argument is: Here is the universe, you've got to account for it some way. The fact that it's here means that there was someone who created it . . . for whatever that argument may be worth.

Teleological is a variation on this. It says we find purpose, and design, and direction, and intent in the universe, and therefore back of it there had to be a purposive, designing, intentional being who brought this about.

The anthropological argument is sometimes called the moral argument. That is that there is goodness and evil in the world and we adjudge good and evil, and yet goodness and evil have no ultimate meaning unless there is an ultimate person who determines good and evil. This argument has really always seemed to have rather sizeable validity to me.

And then, finally, the ontological, which is the most philosophical, and yet philosophers say it is perhaps the most telling. That is the contention that in that I, as a limited fallible human being, can think of God. This I would not be able to do unless God were there to respond to my thought.

15

There they are.

To my mind, despite communism, the question for me, for you, and for the world is not whether God exists, but *what God is like.* The Christian says "The God I believe in *is my Almighty Father, who created heaven and earth."*

We do distort the meaning and the purpose of the Creed when we stop at the point, *I believe in God,* but we do not distort when we pause after the next phrase, when we say, *I believe in God, the Father.*

For, quite literally, to understand that designation is to make the rest of the Creed a superfluous commentary.

As I have said in the communicants' class when I was teaching your youngsters,
> and as I have said to many of you as individuals when you were planning to unite with this church on profession of faith,
> > as I have said from this pulpit in the past and will say again . . . if
> > > for some reason or other we had to lose all of everything that Jesus said except two words, I think we could yet salvage the whole situation. We would take his injunction, "When you pray, say *Our Father"* and we would grasp those two words, *Our Father,* and hold on to them for dear life, indeed dear life, literally said.

I think we would have preserved the essence; for Jesus' whole ministry was a commentary on those two words.

Jesus said, in effect, that our conception of God must ultimately be so limited because of our limited little minds. We might as well recognize that if we can grasp God as a Father that this is as close as we can get. If we will take human fatherhood and thrust it up just as high and as exalted as we can possibly get it and then think of the relationship of that kind of father and his son, we have come as close to God Almighty as we can possibly come in conception.

Sometimes we think that we get further than that in our scientific and pseudo-scientific day when we think of God and his great

16

mechanical powers and influences, and so forth and so on. And we really haven't gotten any closer at all—we've gotten further away.

I was impressed with a little cartoon that I saw in *The New Yorker* just this week . . . maybe some of you saw it. It shows a tremendous computer, as it is many times shown in *The New Yorker* magazine. And here's the guy sitting at the machine, who has been working it like mad. And standing by him is the boss, I guess, who now has the final figures that he's holding, and this is the caption:

"Amazing! It would have taken 4,000 mathematicians 4,000 years to make a mistake like this."

You see, it's still the mathematician, and it would indeed take the mathematicians to make a mistake like that because the mathematician still far surpasses the machine.

So, no matter what changes we have in our culture,
     no matter how people change,
          no matter how our environment changes,
               still at long last there will never become a time
               when at the ultimate exaltation of human relation-
               ship we don't see the supremacy of the final relation-
               ship between a good father and a beloved son.

We shall never pass or surpass Jesus saying . . . "When you pray, say *Our Father.*"

God the Father Almighty.

And that word *Almighty.* To me it's nice, and sonorous, and classical. I always get just a little emotional punch when I say the word *Almighty.* It means the same thing, I guess, as all-powerful, but to me the word *all-powerful* is a contentious little word, an argumentative word. And when somebody says to me that God is all-powerful, then with my little corrupted mind, I start going around trying to find some way to argue with the word and to think of something that God can't do—
     like God can't make yesterday not to have been
          or God can't make a stick with one end
               or something else ridiculous.

But, when I say *God, the Father Almighty,* then there comes to my mind the feeling that no matter what seems to be happening, God is in control of the situation.

No matter how topsy-turvy the world may look to me, to Him He sees it clearly.

No matter how dark the world looks to me, He stands in the light.

No matter how confused I am, it's clear to Him.

No matter how painful this moment may be for me, for Him it has a purpose.

God the Father Almighty, maker of heaven and earth.

To me, that's the lyrical hammer that drives the nail home . . . *maker of heaven and earth.*

Now there is a sense in which that phrase is superfluous if God is almighty. But then, in our day—with its new scientific frontiers— it seems to me that this phrase becomes marvelously timely again, as though we were saying to the scientist:

"Go right ahead exploring the universe all you please, but it's worthwhile for us to remind you that it's not *your* universe, it's not *our* universe, it's *His* universe, and He lets us fiddle with it all we please, but He's watching" . . . and I'm glad!

You remember the story that came out a few years ago told on a Presbyterian elder from the southwest. He was sent as a commissioner to the General Assembly of the Presbyterian Church. He arrived on Monday afternoon, and on Tuesday night he received a telegram which said, "A hailstorm this afternoon destroyed your corn crop. Come home at once."

And he wired back, "If God Almighty wants to use *His* hail to destroy *His* corn, that's *His* business. Attending the General Assembly is *my* business. See you Friday night."

I believe in God the Father Almighty, maker of heaven and earth.

—January 14, 1962

18

AND
IN
JESUS CHRIST

I READ RECENTLY of a missionary who went to Japan and started studying the Japanese language, and after having wrestled with it for awhile, came to the conclusion that this language had been designed by the devil so as to make it impossible to convert any Japanese to Christianity.

Whether this is true, I don't know, but I *do* know, on the other hand, that theologians once talked quite seriously of Hebrew being the language of divinity.

Said these theologians in all seriousness, obviously Hebrew was the language of divinity, for God spoke Hebrew in the Garden of Eden. So then they went on to speculate seriously as to whether or not Hebrew was the language of heaven.

And having gone that far in their speculation, they went on, then, to speculate on whether or not people who got to heaven had to learn Hebrew, or whether they knew it instantaneously just by virtue of arriving in heaven.

For your peace of mind—any of you who have any hopes of getting to heaven—let me reassure you they came to the conclusion you would know Hebrew automatically when you got there.

I found this quite reassuring, because I struggled intermittently and not too enthusiastically with Hebrew for three years in the seminary, and can assure you that if I don't know it when I get to heaven, I'll never know it.

Never having tried Japanese, I can say from my own personal experience, that Hebrew has certain devilish qualities, for as it is written, it has only consonants. The Hebrew language is built on words of just three letters that have a letter tacked to the front sometimes, and a couple to the back . . . but no vowels, only consonants.

In about the fifth century of our era, in that Hebrew was no longer spoken—classical Hebrew was no longer spoken—as a living language, and the pronunciation was lost, the Hebrew scholars worked out a series of dots and dashes to go under the consonants to represent the vowels, because, of course as soon as you reflect on it, you realize that with only the consonants you'd have no idea how a word would be pronounced. These dots and dashes are known among the scholars as the points of Hebrew. When I was in seminary, when we wanted to speak about a really classical scholar, of the ultimate order, we said, "That guy reads unpointed Hebrew."

Jesus wrote unpointed Hebrew. As a matter of fact, Jesus was doubtless trilingual. When He and the other youngsters ran around the streets of Nazareth, He spoke Hebrew, of course, as His native tongue, probably Aramaic of the day, sort of a corruption of classical Hebrew.

In addition to that, doubtless He spoke the language that was necessary to know in order to get along in the world, the language of the Roman conqueror, which was Latin. And, in addition to that, doubtless Jesus spoke the language of all literature of the day . . . and that was Greek.

So He was most probably trilingual.

When Mary, at the close of the day, would come to the cottage door and call Jesus off the street where He had been playing, to come in to His dinner, she called Him, not Jesus, but Joshua, for that was His name.

20

That was His Hebrew name.

She may have said—talking about vowels a minute ago—we're not quite sure, she may have called Him Jeshua, for the consonants would be the same in either instance. But Joshua was a very common name in Jesus' day—Joshua's day—because of the Old Testament hero. The name means "Salvation is from God," and "Jesus" is the Greek-Latin form of the word "Joshua."

So, then, interestingly enough, the two or three times when Joshua from the Old Testament is referred to in the New Testament, he's called Jesus.

For us, the name Jesus has gotten to be identified only with the Man from Nazareth. Those of you who are more widely traveled than I happen to be, and have spent some time in Latin countries, tell me of the shock that one feels when on the street he hears the name "Jesus" used over and over again as a common name, whereas in our own tradition it's confined to the usage of the Man from Nazareth. When it's so used—because the name Jesus or Josuha was His very earthful, earthy name—we use the name Jesus to refer to His earthly ministry.

In contrast, the word "Christ" is not a name, but a title, a designation. It means "The Annointed One." We think of Christ as we think of Him in His divine role, so that getting the feel of the names, you and I customarily—when we think of the man of Galilee walking along the shores of the seaside—would think of Jesus, and speak of Jesus. When we think of Him who is exalted and sitting on the right hand of God the Father, we think of Christ, and speak of Christ. But when we think of that man on the cross, playing this profoundly dual role, we might very appropriately speak of Jesus or of Christ . . . or might say Jesus Christ.

Now having introduced these two words, *Jesus* and *Christ,* let me step aside for a moment to orient us as to where we are.

Last Sunday we began a series of sermons on the Apostles' Creed . . . a series which is to run, with perhaps a break here and there, up until the Easter season. And we said that the Apostles' Creed —of course not having been written by the Apostles, but traditionally assigned to them—is one of the oldest creeds of Christendom. It's called an ecumenical creed, because it's used by the three branches of the church, the Protestant, the Roman Catholic, and the Eastern Orthodox. Probably it does go in its original form back into the second century.

Last Sunday we spoke about the opening words: *I believe in God the Father Almighty, Maker of heaven and earth.*

We move forward, then, in this series, and I should like to ask you to either take the card which is in the pew there, or look at your hymnal on page 53, at the wording of the Creed for just a moment.

If you're looking at the card which is there in the pew, you'll notice that it's divided into paragraphs, and that far and away the longest paragraph is the second, and this whole paragraph has to do with Jesus Christ, by far the largest segment of the Creed. Now looking in the back of the hymnal, you'll see that it's not broken up into paragraphs, but beginning with the third line, *And in Jesus Christ,* and going on down to the line which begins, *I believe in the Holy Ghost . . .* all of those lines have to do with Jesus Christ.

Let me just say them through:

"And in Jesus Christ His only Son, our Lord; who was conceived by the Holy Ghost; born of the Virgin Mary; suffered under Pontius Pilate; was crucified, dead, and buried; the third day He rose again from the dead; He ascended into heaven, and sitteth on the right hand of God the Father Almighty; from thence He shall come to judge the quick and the dead."

It's quite proper that the largest segment of the Creed should have to do with the person and work of Jesus Christ, because at long last, Christianity is about Christ.

This is as we would expect, and as I said last Sunday, originally the Creed was used as a baptismal formula. After the catechumen —the one who was being instructed in Christianity—received instruction for weeks, and sometimes for months, he was ready to be inducted into full Christian membership, by baptism. As one of the last acts of his instruction, he would be taught verbally— because it was not written down—the Creed, perhaps very much in this form as we now have it; sort of secret-like, maybe, because other religious sects had secret creeds and secret words, perhaps because they didn't want it to be distorted.

22

In any event, the first time the Creed was said publicly was as the person received baptism, and thereafter, the Creed was sort of his password or his open sesame into the church whenever he entered it.

This morning we're going to confine our comments to Jesus Christ —all that we're going to talk about are these words: *And in Jesus Christ His only Son, our Lord.*

We have spoken of Jesus as Hebrew, Joshua being His common name. We have spoken of Christ as being a title, "The Annointed One." The word Christ, is just a Greek word coming from the original Greek word χριω which means to annoint, so you can see "Chrio"—Christ.

Over against this we have this Old Testament conception of the Annointed One and the word there is the Hebrew word *Maseeah* or *Messiah*. So, Christ and Messiah are the same word.

If we would orient ourselves we would say the Latin-Greek name of Jesus is Jesus the Christ, the Hebrew would be Joshua the Messiah.

Though you are familiar with the concept of the Messiah, let me speak on it just a moment, because of its significance for us.

Characteristic of primitive peoples is a belief in a golden age long ago . . . that is, of always looking back. The good old days were the best times of all, and since then things have disintegrated and will probably never be as good again.

Unique with the Hebrews—I don't know of any other people who always looked forward—was their conviction that the golden age lay ahead. There would come a time when God would send His own Annointed One, who would come to earth, or would appear on earth, and who would bring in the golden age for the Hebrews —the Lord's day.

Throughout Hebrew history they were looking for the Maseeah, the Messiah, the Annointed One, who would come to bring in the golden age. As I say, this is rather unique in the philosophy of history. We take that over into our Christian tradition, so that the Hebrew-Christian tradition—unique so far as I know in the world

—gives history the direction of an arrow being shot down through time to a target.

For the Christian, the target date is the return of Christ, the ultimate day in human history. The Jews look for the Messiah to come; we look for the Messiah who has come to return.

And when you want to explain Western civilization, you cannot explain it apart from this arrow direction of history moving towards a target. I won't enlarge on that this morning, but I should like to on some other occasion.

Having talked about Jesus Christ, let's pass on to this phrase, *His only Son*. The word *only* is "monogenes"—"only begotten." The Greeks and the Hebrews contemporaneous with apostolic Christianity, used, as we might use, street parlance wherein they talked about the son of God . . . the sons of God . . . or the sons of the gods . . . you know, in which a pagan might say, "This is a very noble man, indeed a son of the gods."

So in order to distinguish what the Christian was talking about, right in the New Testament and on down into Christian history we have monogenes "the only begotten of God" which means the unique Son of God. And in time, then, Son of God comes to be an expression used only in relationship with Christ.

How can this phrase 'Son of God" have any reality for us as twentieth century Christians?

Obviously, the word *Son* has to be used in some descriptive sense; it cannot be used in the literal sense because it cannot be used in the same physical frame of reference as we use the relationship *son*.

I wrestled with what I would do about this next section of this sermon. I'm going to do as I did at the 9:30 service with the recognition that here we will be wrestling with a difficult concept, a mystery, if you please.

I have no aspiration at all to try to explain, but only to present that which is pretty basic to our Christian theology . . . our Christology. I ask you to follow me, as best you can, not because I am learned—I am not learned—but we are intelligent together.

24

We have to wrestle with this and try to hold it in our minds, so follow me now as best you can.

You and I as Christians do not believe that the Son of God came into being on the first Christmas Eve, when the babe of Bethlehem was born. We believe that part of the eternal nature of God became flesh, that this was the incarnation . . . this was when God in some mysterious sense became man. This is not just some idea I dreamed up; it was right in the Scripture which we read. Let me just read this much again:

"In many and various ways God spoke of old to our fathers by the prophets, but in these last days He has spoken to us by a Son, [listen now] whom He appointed the heir of all things, [and then this phrase] through whom He also created the world."

This is not unique to the book of Hebrews, it's several places in the New Testament.

This idea of God's creating the world through one aspect of His nature which became incarnate, became flesh, the Greeks and the Hebrews—these were the two cultures that converged—had a way to handle this. For both of them had this conception: that God as God is adequate in Himself, God doesn't need anything . . .

But for some mysterious, strange reason God decided to create the universe. And when God created the universe it was as though he turned a part of His nature out toward His universe so that this part could be comprehended by the universe; the universe couldn't understand all of God . . . only this aspect. This aspect of God both the Hebrews and the Greeks called the *wisdom* of God. So said they—not trying to explain it—this wisdom became flesh in Jesus Christ.

I have tried to find some analogy for this, to try to give it a little bit of reality for myself. I don't have a very good analogy . . . I'm going to give you the best I could come up with.

When I was a youngster coming along through grade school, I had as one of my characteristics that of developing a deep attachment for my teacher—my school teacher—almost instantaneously, as I moved from grade to grade. In wanting to have a warm

25

identification with her, I can remember grade after grade after grade how I would sit there in school, and after school
    and think of her as being my school teacher . . .
        and then thinking of how much of her life was *outside* of school
            and wondering what her home was like
                how she acted when she was out of school
                    the things she liked to do
                        how she and I would talk if we were not in school
                            and so forth and so on . . .
all of these speculations of a youngster.

So see, I had this in-school relationship with her, but I could dream of this out-of-school relationship.

The analogy there would be God as He's related to His universe "in-school." This aspect of God would be God as we see Him through the incarnation, recognizing all of this out-of-school relationship which is pretty much unknown to us.

I don't propose that you have a nice, clear understanding of this. If you do, you're better off than I am. But it is necessary for us as Christians to face the implications of this pre-incarnation of Christ, that the Son of God is eternal with the Father.

Now this is a mystery. You can't get it clearly in your mind. You and I as twentieth century science-oriented and pseudoscience-oriented people don't like mysteries, and we don't like to accept them.

Well, I don't want any hocus-pocus in my religion either, but humility and intellectual honesty call for us to recognize that there are concepts, not just in the realm of religion, which we cannot grasp.

Let me give you just two illustrations.

Philosophy wrestles, as does science, with whether or not this is a limited or an unlimited universe.

How can you possibly conceive either one?

A universe with limits? Then what's just two inches beyond the limit? Or without limits? And, yet, how can this be? So we can't actually conceive either a limited or an unlimited universe, but we can wrestle with the concept.

The same thing about human personality. You think you understand what human personality is until you try to stand off and say what makes human personality, and then you'll find out it's the slipperiest concept you ever tried to wrestle with.

There are things which are too mysterious for us to be able to grasp because of our limited intelligence. Nevertheless they can be true. So be it then said about the eternal Christ as a part of the eternal God-head. *I believe in Jesus Christ His only Son.*

Now this last phrase, *Our Lord.* Notice that you begin with *I* in the Creed, and then without warning move over to *Our.* To be consistent linguistically, one would say, "I believe in Jesus Christ, His only Son, My Lord." But it's not *my* it's *our* for you see, the Creed says—and I think theologically properly— that you and I may not say *"My* Lord" with any reality, until we have learned to say *"Our* Lord." Lord, of course, means "ruler of life."

There is a real sense in which one can not be a solitary Christian . . . we can only be Christians together. And it's interesting, I think, to recognize in passing how this has come up in literary productions.

Christian men have on several occasions built a desert island where they would start life again. For example, the story of Robinson Crusoe. And, yet, interestingly enough, as soon as DeFoe gets Robinson Crusoe on the island by himself, then DeFoe has to get out and find the good man Friday to come in to be converted to Christianity, and to create the Christian community.

Then, when we find the Swiss Family Robinson—that deeply loved story that so many of us have read as a family book—here is the creation of the Christian community.

Or that play that came out some years ago, "The Admirable Chrighton"—the butler who was a Christian who created the Christian community.

Somehow or other, Christianity can be Christianity only in communities.

After we have said "Our Lord," then we can say "My Lord."

Jesus Christ the ruler of *our* lives, hence the ruler of *my* life.

I think that if my Christianity arrives at the place where it should, then something warm ought to happen down inside whenever I say "My Lord." There ought to be some warmth there, there ought to be some sense of gratitude and dedication.

Because I always try to be honest with you from this pulpit, I can say to you that here from time to time I can feel a little surge of this warmth, but not what I would like.

Here's what I would like, if I can draw an analogy.

Let me say prefatorily, that I love our nation as it is with its form of government. I do not want to change it. But, from time to time, when I talk with one of our English friends—and England also, of course, is a great democracy—and I mention the Royal Family, I elicit from that Englishman a sudden warmth. It doesn't make any difference what sort of an Englishman he is—and from what I know of Englishmen, sudden warmth doesn't come frequently—but you mention, you just mention the Queen. Or in a previous reign, the King, or the Prince. You mention anything about the Royal Family and you feel this little surge of warmth.

I could wish that somehow or other in my Christianity that whenever I say "Our Lord" I could feel something of a little comparable surge of warmth that the Englishman feels when he says "Our Royal Family."

I believe in Jesus Christ His only Son, Our Lord.

—January 21, 1962

CRUCIFIED, DEAD, AND BURIED

[*This phrase in the Creed was treated in a communion meditation, which was not recorded, and therefore could not be reproduced for inclusion in this book.*]

BORN

OF

THE VIRGIN

In that the New Testament speaks more than once of Jesus' brothers—at least twice in Matthew, and in Paul's letter to the Galatians—it seems that the Church for over 200 years never considered anything to the contrary than that in Joseph's and Mary's household there were other children born following Jesus, who were reared in this household with him as his brothers.

As a matter of fact, more than one of the early church fathers used the evidence of Jesus' brothers to prove in the early theological controversies—when there was contesting about the nature of Christ—the fact that Jesus had brothers as evidence of Jesus' humanity.

During this time, the Church seems to have accorded no particular place of honor to Mary, other than love and respect. Then in the fourth century—at the beginning of the fourth century, around three hundred and five or six, I believe—there came the conversion of the Emperor Constantine, and the persecutions of the Church ceased.

It became acceptable and proper to be a Christian.

The Christians came out of the catacombs and set about their business of living in the Roman Empire. And at this point, the theological arguments set in for sure, as now the Church turned its mind to resolving the theological enigmas that laced their way through Christian thinking.

One of the side effects of Constantine's conversion, and the end of martyrdom, was a rather rapid rise of hero worship of the martyrs. And with this came the gathering of the relics of the martyrs, their clothing, and their bones, and any of the instruments that they had held. Then came the celebrations of the days of the martyrs' deaths as their spiritual birthdays, and hence the Saint's Days, so that, rather rapidly, the whole calendar was filled with Saint's Days.

This was the period when Mariolatry—or the adoration of the Blessed Virgin—got going with great velocity, and gathered momentum as it went along. Since there was very little or nothing in the New Testament to hinder the imagination, the Church now with this new area of speculation, and this rather exciting area of speculation, seized on exaltation of Mary with vigorous enthusiasm.

One of the first steps in this exultation was to declare the perpetual virginity of Mary; that is, following Jesus' miraculous conception and birth, Mary never had any other children.

The several genuine references in the New Testament to Jesus' family could be easily accounted for. And I think with not any great stretching of one's imagination, I can see how it would be accepted, that Joseph's children, as reflected in the New Testament, were by a previous marriage.

These children were older than Jesus. Joseph had been previously married and his wife had died, and Mary was his second wife. This was pure speculation, so far as I can see, but certainly not any very wild thesis.

The adoration of the Virgin, therefore gathering momentum, continued right on down to the time of the Reformation, and then has continued in the Roman Church on down to the present, until most recently—within the last decade, I believe—there has been the declaration by the Pope of the dogma that is now a part of Roman Catholic theology, of the Bodily Assumption of the Virgin

. . . that at the time of Mary's death, her body was not corrupted, but was lifted physically into Heaven.

I'm not an authority on Mariolatry, and so I may be remiss here, or in error in making this statement, but as I understand it, the next step would be, and may become, that of declaring Mary to be co-redemptrix with Christ; that is that thereby she would be declared to be able to forgive sins in her own right, rather than only as a mediator between man and Christ.

In any event—in summarizing how one branch of the Church now deals with its relationship with Mary—it can be said that the essence of Mariolatry lies in her being referred to by our Roman Catholic brethren not as Jesus' mother, but as Theotocos . . . that is, as the Mother of God, which, as you know, is apparent in the history of the Church for the first time, I believe, in either the third or the fourth century, so far as I am aware. It is not a Scriptural designation.

The aim of this recital is to point to the fact that on one end of the spectrum of Christian theology the role of Jesus' mother has been exalted and enlarged so as to make many Christians feel that Mary has actually replaced Christ in the love and loyalty of many Christians.

Be that as it may, let me leave it there for a moment in order to remind you of the obvious. That is that we are in the midst of a series of sermons on the Apostles' Creed, a creed that is the oldest that we have in Christendom in any filled-out form, doubtless going back, in its original form, to the second century. It continues down into your and my day, and into our morning worship as a continuation of a statement of the Christian faith, being one of the few statements that can be shared in its totality by the three branches of the Church. At their worship this morning, Presbyterians, Roman Catholics, and Greek Orthodox, shared this creed, at least by that much, binding together the broken body of our Lord, Jesus Christ.

Since Christianity at long last is all about Christ, the largest portion of the creed, as it should, deals with the person and the work of Christ. For after beginning, as the Creed does, with these words: *I believe in God the Father Almighty, Maker of heaven and earth,* then the Creed moves in its largest paragraph, and its longest paragraph, to deal with the person and the work of Christ: "and in Jesus Christ His only Son our Lord; who was conceived by the Holy Ghost; born of the Virgin Mary; suffered under Pontius Pilate; was crucified, dead, and buried; the third day He rose again from the dead; He ascended into heaven; and sitteth on the right hand of God the Father Almighty; from thence He shall come to judge the quick and the dead."

We are working our way through the Creed, and come now to the parallel phrases, *Who was conceived by the Holy Ghost; born of the Virgin Mary.*

This phrase, *conceived by the Holy Ghost,* means obviously— as we read each year in our Christmas story—that Jesus was conceived by a direct act of God, and hence the resulting phrase, *born of the Virgin Mary.*

I have said that on one end of the theological spectrum—as represented by the Roman branch of the Church—Mary has been exalted into a role that many feel is actually contesting with the role of Christ.

Now let's go back to the other end of the spectrum.

The denial of the virgin birth of Jesus is by far and away the most common first break with conventional orthodoxy.

To indicate what I mean by this, if Roman Catholic theology represents the far right—the most conservative swing of the theological pendulum—and if Unitarianism represents the left of the theological spectrum, of course, that puts me, as a self-righteous Presbyterian, right in the middle, which of course is the true position where one stands tolerant of deviations, but smugly assured of his own sound but gracious orthodoxy.

So, we have Roman Catholics on the right, Unitarians on the left, and us Presbyterians here in the middle.

The first swing of the needle from the center of theology and center of orthodoxy—I'm trying to use a word in bad repute in good repute here—let's act like orthodoxy's a good word for a few minutes (I think it is) . . . let's so use it—here in the center

33

of orthodoxy the first swing of the needle to the left is frequently —and more frequently than anything else, I think—the denying of Jesus' virgin birth, accompanied always of course, by a denial of the verbal inerrancy of Scripture.

By verbal inerrancy, we mean the belief that the Bible is exactly as God dictated it, that there are no mistakes of any kind in the Bible.

It can be seen that to contend about the virgin birth is also to have to contend about verbal inerrancy, for the Gospels of Matthew and Luke so clearly teach the virgin birth that there is no way to deny it, except by saying that there are errors in the Bible.

There are several things I want to say all at once, and I don't know how quite to put them in logical order. Maybe the best thing to do is for me to start by stating my own position as simply and as directly as I can, and to go from there. To keep it simple and direct, let me say first *what* I believe with little if any commentary on *why* I believe it . . . only say enough of the *why* to explain the *what*.

I believe in the virgin birth.

That is, I accept as historical fact the story of Jesus' birth as given to us in Matthew and Luke. The reason I believe it is because it is in the Bible, and really that's, I think, probably the *only* reason why I hold to it that strongly.

I want to say this next:

I do not believe that you have to accept the virgin birth to be a Christian.

If that were required, we could not be sure of but two Christians in the New Testament, Matthew and Luke. For neither Mark nor John, even by implication, suggest the virgin birth. Paul nowhere mentions, even by implication, the virgin birth
>nor does Peter
>>nor does the writer of the Hebrews
>>>nor any other New Testament writer.

So, if commitment to the virgin birth has to be the sole shibboleth by which one is declared a Christian, then we have only two assured Christians in the New Testament.

34

As conceived by many fine Christians, and as many fine Christians are convinced—and this I have said—there are a multitude of magnificent Christians who exalt Mary, far beyond the position to which I would exalt her.

So, on the other hand, I think that there are millions—certainly multitudes—of fine Christians who find it impossible to accept the Virgin birth
and these are not crackpots
they're not left-wingers
they're not anything but real conservative . . .
(And once again I'd like to use the word conservative in a constructive sense) real conservative *Christians*.

Somewhere about here, maybe I should say what I believe about the Bible, for I have said that one's commitment to the virgin birth, and one's commitment to the Bible, must at least in a negative sense, run along together.

However, I won't take time to talk about my belief about the Bible this morning, because it would be too diversionary and too involved.

It is interesting to me that the Apostles' Creed does not even mention the Bible. As for myself, I believe that there are a multitude, and variety of kinds of errors in the Bible. But when I say that there are errors in the Bible, that does not mean that I am liberal; that only means that I am a good Biblical scholar. It's when *other* people say there are errors in the Bible that they're *liberal!* In *my* instance it's only sound Biblical scholarship. So it all depends on who's saying it.

But I'll talk about the Bible in another frame of reference at another time, because either it should be only touched on or enlarged upon, so let me let it stay there for the moment.

The Bible has survived without my commenting on it for some time, and probably will survive until I do.

Whether one believes in or doesn't believe in the virgin birth, let us see what is the purpose that is supposed to be served by this doctrine. I think that we can agree on what it is *designed* to do whether we believe it or not.

35

The story of Jesus' virgin birth is designed to demonstrate and protect His *uniqueness*. In the stream of human history, there has been no one like Him before, and there is no one destined to come like Him after.

The virgin birth points to Jesus' vertical relationship with God Almighty. This is to keep from running into the position where one says, "Here is a good man, here is another good man, a little bit better, a little bit better, a little bit better." At the pinnacle, one encounters this man Jesus, on both sides people just below Him, who might reach up and touch His shoulder, or even might stand up to His brow line. Therefore, there might be others of any given degree of goodness who come on down into human history, and perhaps on another pinnacle somewhere one will stand equal with Jesus."

As over against this, the doctrine of the virgin birth says, "Jesus is absolutely unique in human history; that He is God's act directly for mankind."

To the extent that the acceptance of the virgin birth is the only way to preserve the uniqueness of Christ, to that extent exactly would I contend for the virgin birth, for I am convinced that the uniqueness of Jesus is the very *yes* or *no* of the Christian faith.

In so saying, I feel that I am on very sound ground, for this is the contention of the Presbyterian Church on the one hand, and the World Council of Churches on the other.

When you joined the Presbyterian Church, you committed yourself, theologically—and I think exclusively—in terms of necessity of commitment to a recognition of Jesus' role as being unique in His relationship to mankind. This is the basis on which the Christian Church at New Delhi bespoke once again its own unity, the basis on which the world Church is built.

But as for me, it is easy to see how someone can hold strongly to the uniqueness of Christ without holding to the virgin birth.

To me, one can be committed to Jesus Christ as Lord and Savior, and as to God's unique gift to mankind, without this gift having come about by means of a virgin birth.

So then it comes down to this: to me whereas it is not critical for one's ultimate relationship with God Almighty, the virgin birth is important as it protects verbally what I believe to be the ultimate spiritual reality in the world . . . that God Almighty acted directly for man in the person of Jesus Christ as he did nowhere else in human history,

and that this is the single most important fact in the world.

Hence, I am making the declaring of that fact, the proclaiming of that fact, my whole career.

To the extent, then
 that proclaiming
  and protecting
   and pronouncing the uniqueness of Christ for the
   affairs of men rests in the virgin birth . . .
to that extent I consider the virgin birth as a focal doctrine of the Christian faith.

February 11, 1962

SUFFERED
UNDER
PONTIUS PILATE

JESUS STOOD BEFORE THE GOVERNOR, and the governor asked Him, "Are you the king of the Jews?"

And Jesus said to him, "You have said so."

But when He was accused by the chief priests and elders, He made no answer.

Then Pilate said to Him, "Do you not hear how many things they testify against you?"

But He gave him no answer, not even to a single charge so that the governor wondered greatly.

At the feast, the governor was accustomed to release for the crowd any one prisoner whom they wanted, and they had then a notorious prisoner called Barabas.

So when they had gathered, Pilate said to them, "Whom do you want me to release for you, Barabas, or Jesus who is called Christ?" For he knew that it was out of envy that they had delivered Him up. Besides, while he was on the judgment seat, his wife sent word to him saying, "Have nothing to do with that righteous man for I have suffered much over him today in a dream."

The chief priests and the elders persuaded the people to ask for Barabas, and destroy Jesus. The governor again said to them, "Which of the two do you want me to release for you?"

And they said, "Barabas."

Pilate said to them, "Then what shall I do with Jesus who is called Christ?"

They all said, "Let Him be crucified!"

And he said, "Why, what evil has He done?"

But they shouted all the more, "Let him be crucified!"

So when Pilate saw that he was gaining nothing, but rather that a riot was beginning, he took water and washed his hands before the crowd, saying, "I am innocent of this Man's blood, see ye to it yourselves."

There are many articles and some books that have been written about the cosmology of the Bible. I have read some of the articles and at least one of the books, and by cosmology, this is what we mean:

What did the physical universe look like to the men in Bible times?

What world view did they have?

What was their physical picture of the universe?

I know that what I shall describe is commonplace, but we need to pull it back into focus for some other things that we want to say.

The view throughout the Bible—all the way from Abraham down to Paul, a period of about 2,000 years—is pretty much the same, so we can talk together of the Biblical world view of Abraham and Paul.

It was something like this: the universe was in three obvious layers. Here was heaven up here with the stars and the moon and the sun, and beyond this heaven, of course, would be the physical heaven where God was. And then here was the flat earth, and down below the earth would be where hell was, or the nether world. The earth is flat, and square. The land which makes up the earth is surrounded by water. How thick the earth is isn't said specifically, but it's thick enough for nobody to fall through if he wanted to dig down a ways. But it's not so thick but what the waters down under the earth could break up through the earth, say at the time of the flood.

They were quite aware, were these men, of the actions of the heavenly bodies, and studied the movement of the sun, and the moon, and the stars. They considered of course, that these things swung around the earth, and they were not too sure how they got down under, but they came back up, and they were confident, of course, that this earth—this square earth—was the center of the universe, and that everything swung around it . . . and that the universe was centered on this world, this earth.

Let me leave that for a moment, and make another leap, and then come back to this matter of cosmology.

The great scientific revolution—which characterizes the last several hundred years of our Western culture—started about the same time as men began to explore the world, to make the trips around the world, about the same time as the Protestant Reformation, and the Renaissance. All of these things began to move along together.

As you and I look back upon that period, we are not very happy with what we discover about either the Protestant or the Roman Catholic Church, and how they acted. And on many occasions we are embarrassed, particularly with the manner in which the Church reacted against scientific advancement. From the time of Copernicus and Galileo—as soon as this scientific advancement got under way—the Church started fighting a rear guard action against science.

Right on down to mine and your day and the battle of Clarence Darrow and William Jennings Bryan and the Scopes trial . . . always the Church fighting and battling against scientific advancement.

As Copernicus and Galileo insisted that the world was round, that the sun stood still, and that the earth swung around the sun, so the Church just at this point was so extremely angry as to say, "Either you have to recant, or you give up your life."

And so the Church yelled in anguish at every scientific advancement on down to the Scopes trial in Tennessee, in our day and time, where the Church was battling evolution.

40

Why has the Church so often battled against scientific advancement? It's certainly not justified, but on reflection I think that it's understandable. It's my feeling that all of the way the Church felt like it was battling for the life of its people . . . that the Church, though it did not voice it, had the feeling that every scientific pronouncement made the simple Christian faith harder to hold on to. And I think that there is a real sense in which the Church had a genuine insight.

As I say, it was not justifiable, but I think it's understandable, because I do think that every pushing back of the scientific frontier has made the so-called simple Christian faith harder to hold on to.

All right, now let me leave that for a moment and digress.

In case there is still someone who is not aware of it, we are in the middle of a series of sermons on the Apostles' Creed, this oldest creed in Christendom that manages in its being recited to pull all of Christendom into the one family of God in Christ Jesus.

Today we're dealing with these words concerning Christ: *suffered under Pontius Pilate; was crucified, dead, and buried.*

But before dealing with those words, I'd like to point out something that a number of people have asked me to point out . . . to remind you that next Sunday we have a specific sermon coming up, and if I were trying to be a sensationalist I would urge you to please come back to church next Sunday so that together we can go to hell.

Next Sunday we are going to descend into the inferno, where the Apostles' Creed says, *He descended into hell,* and we Presbyterians stopped saying it a generation or so ago. A number of you have asked me, as I say, to indicate when this sermon would take place, and so we will be speaking on this aspect of the creed on next Sunday.

Now back to the words, *suffered under Pontius Pilate; crucified, dead, and buried.*

Let's see where we are.

We have said that in Biblical times there was this simple cosmology of dividing the universe into up here where the heavens are, then the earth, then under the earth . . . three layers. We have said that the Church put on a constant battle with scientific advancement of the last several hundred years, and that this scientific advancement seemingly has made it harder to hold onto the Christian faith. Well, let's move on from there.

This is what we mean by the essence of the Christian theology that is harder to hold onto. That on a certain Friday afternoon, in a certain, specific year, at a particular place on this little planet, there was a certain, specific man who was tortured to death on a cross, and that that specific act, of that man being put to death, changed God's relationship with man, and man's relationship with God.

I submit to you that it was much easier to believe that one, specific, historical act of one man's death was designed by God to change human history, man's relationship with God, and God's relationship with man . . .

I submit to you—without trying to be smart-alecky at all—that it was much *easier* to believe *that* when we had heaven *not so far away,* up here in a nice *specific* place . . . and a nice, big, flat earth.

Without trying to be clever, back in those days it was not nearly as far from heaven to Jerusalem as it is now.

We do ourselves—and I think God Almighty—only justice when we face the fact that the thrusting back of the scientific frontiers of the universe thousands and millions of light years, so that now we don't even know (as I was saying several weeks ago) . . . we can't even picture whether we're talking about a limited or an unlimited universe, whatever that may mean.

This receded frontier makes it much more difficult to see that act on Friday afternoon to be what it was made out to be two thousand years ago.

As a matter of fact, one might ask, how *can* we believe in historical Christianity today? That is what we are wrestling with now. I might say to you, that what is *more* important is *why* should we believe in it? And this I think I can tell you in part.

42

Since Biblical times and pre-Biblical times, man's pattern of the universe, as we say, has radically changed . . . but hear this. Since Biblical times, in Biblical times, and down until today, man's *moral* problems have not changed. We speak of the world's view between Abraham and Paul as having undergone no change of consequence; they had the same world view . . . and that ours had radically changed.

But note this. In the four thousand years since Abraham, down through the time of the apostle Paul, and down through today, mankind has not dreamed up one single new personal problem—not one! Nor has mankind been able to drop out of the category one single sin.

This morning when I go home after church, and pick up the morning paper—which I haven't done yet . . . haven't had a chance to see it—I know that I'm not sticking my neck out, if I say to you, that as I read it I will find—and you and I are not subjected to sensational journalism here in the Washington area—that in our very staid and properly edited papers, I will find in that issue today murder, theft, lying, adultery, mob violence, official corruption, and a multitude of other moral infamies, crimes, and distortions.

And as I read the list, I can say to myself, "Abraham, four thousand years ago, knew about, and experienced, and witnessed every single one of them."

Then I can go to the Bible and work through the Bible anywhere I please and go through all of the crimes, and sins, and distortions, and mismanagements of mankind, and I will find that there is not one single sin of man listed in the Bible that we don't still carry on in our society today.

They had a few variations on sin that seem to have added a little bit of attractiveness to the day, and we've dropped some of the variations, maybe, and added some of our own, but not very much at that.

So I am reminding you that man's view of the universe has changed radically
    and man's moral conduct has changed not at all
        and that Christianity has to do with man's moral conduct.

43

Therefore, there is nothing outmoded, there's nothing old-fashioned, about the problem with which Christianity deals, because it is with us today just as much, and in just the same form as ever.

Further, if the Creed has any part therein which contributes anything to an understanding of, or resolution of, the moral problem of mankind, we do well to listen to it again. The Creed says, *I believe in Jesus Christ, who suffered under Pontius Pilate.*

What in the world can that phrase, *suffered under Pontius Pilate,* contribute to our lives? To me, that phrase is the dateline of God's dealing with man.

In his ultimate communication with mankind—as must be done with all letters for them to have any meaning—God puts on there a specific day, *when Pontius Pilate was governor.* This is just as much a day in history as to speak of the time when John F. Kennedy was President of the United States, or Frankie Mann was Mayor of Alexandria. This is the single historic reference in the Creed which nails down a dateline.

I had occasion recently to encounter, in a rather interesting fashion, how important a dateline can be. Allie and I love our Christmas cards, and we are sort of like squirrels about them. We're afraid you all won't send any next year, so we keep all we have, and from time to time we go back and look at them again. A few years have gone by now—and the space was getting to be at something of a premium—so the other night Allie had out a tremendous stack of Christmas cards, going through them again . . . reading the notes, and so forth and so on.

I was sitting there enjoying this recounting of some previous years, and then, sort of apropos nothing, Allie asked me . . . "Are you aware how many Christmas cards you have to look at before you find one with a date on it?"

I had never thought about it. Of course we had thrown away the envelopes, so it was just a matter of looking at the cards.

She said, "I have a stack of cards here, and I've turned through card, after card, after card, before I found one with a date on it. And until I find out what year it is, then this is just Christmas in general."

You think how strange it would be along about July or August to find a card without any date on it and just mail it to your friends, saying . . . "I wish you Merry Christmas and Happy New Year in general from now on."

A card only takes on meaning as at some spot a person sits down and writes one with a date on it. It says the Christmas of 1961 . . . this is the one for which I am wishing you a Merry Christmas, and the Happy New Year is for 1962 . . . not just for whatever number of years you may remain on earth.

So the dateline becomes specifically important, and the messages which are conveyed have meaning, have reality, only as they get tied in with a date.

I say it to you that *suffered under Pontius Pilate* is the dateline of God's delivering his final communication historically to mankind. *Suffered under Pontius Pilate* means that God did not act in general for mankind, that God acted specifically within human history to solve man's problem in human history.

Man does not stand *in general;* man stands *specifically, in human history*. This is where the problem is, and this is where God steps in to solve it. For you see, man's problem is
> not how to make things
>> not where he is going
>>> not what form of transportation he is going to use
>>>> not how many gadgets he has in his hand . . .
Man's problem is how is he going to behave?

That's what Christianity is dealing with, and that's what God Almighty was dealing with on a specific Friday afternoon.

Then what does the fact that Jesus Christ died on a cross on a specific afternoon—a specific Friday afternoon—in history during the time of Pontius Pilate . . . what possible meaning can that have?

It means this: it means that you and I as human beings are supposed to behave towards each other as God was behaving towards mankind in that specific act.

How was God acting?

45

God was thereby demonstrating His self-sacrificing, forgiving love.

Well, why did it actually have to happen?

Why did this specific thing have to take place?

It's because it is the only way that self-sacrificing love could take on reality. For self-sacrificing love can never be demonstrated in general, it can only be demonstrated by a specific act.

Let me tell you a true story.

Several months ago there was a man who happened to come back to Washington who used to be a member of this congregation. He is now living somewhere on the shores of Lake Erie, and I should know the name of the city, but I've forgotten it. It *is* apropos the story that he lives on the shores of Lake Erie.

He came in town on some business and was gracious enough to call me and say, "Let's have lunch together." So I went over . . . as I recall it was over at National Airport. We were sitting there having lunch, catching up on family talk. I was filling him in on our family and so I told him about this tremendous brute we him about Atlas' carryings on in our household. (Atlas is a Chihuahua.)

This friend, George, spoke up and said, "You know, I like dogs very much." This was hardly an original comment designed to shake up anybody, so I accepted this, and he said, "As a matter of fact I have a dog." This once again brought no great resurgence of feeling on my part, and he said, "He is a big old boxer." Well, this also I could still go along with, because I've had a boxer. So he said, "And I love my boxer very much." Still nothing happened down inside. I could picture him going down the street with this handsome brute, with these big massive shoulders, and coming to a corner and reaching down and patting the dog, and so on . . . so this is fine.

He said, "You know, one afternoon I went out sailing on Lake Erie with several friends in a right good-sized sailboat, and it was a right rough afternoon." And he said, "For some season, which I can't remember, I had my boxer along with me." He said, "By the way, do you know that a boxer cannot swim except just a little

46

bit." I said, "Yes, I know that." Having had one, I know they are so heavy, so compact, that they have very little buoyancy, and they drown very easily. He said, "Well I want to be sure that you are aware of this fact, because of what comes next."

He said, "We were out on the boat . . . I was looking over the water, and the waves were breaking over the bow, and all of a sudden I heard some scratching, and I looked around," and he said, "my boxer had fallen overboard." So he said, "I waited for a moment, and dove in right after him. I swam out to him— I had on all my clothes—and I was taking off my clothes as fast as I could, to get off as much of this stuff that was weighing me down."

And he said, "You know, I can still feel those paws as they raked down my chest and drew the blood." So he said, "What I did, I swam away from him and I would tread water, until the dog got exhausted and was about to go under . . . then I would swim up to him and put my arms around him, and hold him to let him rest. And then when he had rested, I would turn him loose, and swim away again."

He said, "Now I don't remember whether I stayed in that water ten minutes or twenty minutes or a half hour . . . I don't know." But he said, "The only thing that I remember is the last time I saw him going under and swam up and put my arms around him . . . and when I came to . . . he and I were on the boat."

You see, self-sacrificial love can't be in general. It has to be at a specific time, at a specific place.

One Friday afternoon, at a specific time, at a specific place, God Almighty dove into the dirty chaos of human life to demonstrate self-sacrificing love. I know it's difficult to believe that today, but it's worth the struggle.

February 18, 1962

HE
DESCENDED
INTO HELL

IN PETER'S FIRST EPISTLE we read these words . . . "Christ has also once suffered for sins, the just for the unjust, that he might bring us to God, being put to death in the flesh, but quickened by the Spirit . . ."

And now listen to these words . . . "In which he went and preached to the spirits in prison who formerly did not obey when God's patience waited in the days of Noah during the building of the ark, in which a few, that is, eight persons, were saved through water." This has been called perhaps the most difficult passage in the whole New Testament and it is on that passage alone that we build our foundation for placing in the Creed these words, *He descended into hell.*

There's one other passage that some have said deals with this same thing. Let me read these words and you can decide for yourselves whether you think they apply. Over in the Letter to the Ephesians, Paul has this passage—Ephesians 4:7 . . .

"But grace was given to each of us, according to the measure of Christ's gift. Therefore it is said, 'When He ascended on high, He led a host of captives, and He gave gifts to men.' " This is a quotation from Psalms . . . "In saying 'He ascended', what does it mean but that He had also descended into the lower parts of the earth? He who descended is He who also ascended far above all the heavens."

Now if you know any more difficult passages in the Scripture, I'd like for you to tell me what they are.

And as I say, on the basis of these verses, the Church has taught that between the Crucifixion and the Resurrection, Jesus went to some place where the unsaved were—some place of the dead—and preached to them. So little did the Church have to go on, and the Church was so unsure as to just who Jesus preached to, and what the outcome was, that this conviction—or rather this doctrine— did not find its way into the Apostles' Creed until the fifth century.

The rest of the Creed had been pretty much put together by the end of the second century—the basic part—but this wasn't put in until the fifth century along with one other phrase that comes along even somewhat later . . . *I believe in the communion of the saints.* We shall be dealing with that at a later time.

Let me pause now to orient ourselves.

We're discussing the Apostles' Creed, the oldest—if not the oldest, *one* of the oldest—statements of our Christian faith put in creedal form, and still shared by the three basic branches of the Christian church—the Protestant, the Roman Catholic, and the Greek Orthodox.

Having worked our way down through various passages, we come now to one which we Presbyterians conventionally omit: *He descended into hell.* Some several generations ago, the Church— the Presbyterian Church and other branches of the Church—looking again at the Creed and its Scriptural foundation, came to the conclusion that this phrase came in so late, and is of such dubious value, that our Assembly recommended, or suggested, that any and all churches who wanted to leave it out, do so.

Those who want to leave it in, certainly are free to do so, and it is not contrary, of course, to Christian doctrine.

All right. Let me leave that for a moment, and move off in another direction, to come back at this same problem.

If there is to be a discussion about what happens to people after they die, it seems to me that one has his choice of three avenues of approach. He can say in the first place, "We don't know what happens to people when they die, therefore I won't try to speculate on it, because I do not have any information, and speculation is futile."

One can say in the second place, *"Since* we do not know what happens to people when they die, we're certainly free to make our own guesses, our own speculations, and our own efforts at determination . . . with the recognition that certainly one man's guess is as good as another. So one can refuse to speculate, or he can say, "I can speculate as much as I please," *or* he can say, "I shall see what the *Bible* has to say, and confine myself to that."

As for myself, I choose to stick with the Bible. And I choose to try to sharpen my convictions and my understanding to the point that I can get any light from the Bible, and to stop at that point, and to believe that beyond that, pure, sheer speculation is probably rather futile.

As to the next step of dealing specifically with the Bible, let me say that if one goes to the Old Testament, he doesn't learn much. It is generally recognized that with the exception of one or two vague references in the Psalms to Sheol, that, for the most part, the Old Testament has nothing to say about what happens to a man after he dies.

It appears that the Hebrews thought that whenever anyone died, his spirit moved to a sort of an indeterminate place called Sheol, in which one was neither particularly dead nor particularly alive. Going to this place had no moral overtones, just everybody who died, went there.

The Hebrews, as we can understand it, had neither any particular fear of, or enthusiasm for, Sheol . . . hence the constant Hebrew prayer that God would give one the gift of long life *here,* and put off as long as possible going to this place called Sheol. So, when we finish reading the Old Testament, we don't know anymore than we know *now* about what happens to a man after he dies.

When we come to the New Testament, this is distinctly a different matter.

50

Let me say to you that it is hard, if not impossible, for you and me to approach the New Testament as though we were reading it for the first time. If we could do so—if we could read the New Testament from cover to cover, as though we had never read it before, and then close the book—I'm convinced that this is the overwhelming impression that we would have concerning what the whole New Testament is all about. We would come away feeling that the whole overall general theme of the New Testament has to do with Jesus of Nazareth, who was God's Appointed One; to live, and to die, and to be resurrected, and that hence, any and all those who acknowledge this Risen Christ to be the Lord of Life, therein and thereby assure themselves of their own life after death.

That for all who claim Christ as Lord there awaits a blissful state of life after death, where one will be directly in God's presence, where one's life will be joyous, and that beyond making this promise, the New Testament shows tremendous restraint in trying to describe what this life will be like.

I repeat, that to me, this is the overall central message of the New Testament, the impression one would come away with if he had never read the New Testament before. And this is stated over and over again with great assurance within the New Testament. *But,* from that point on, very rapidly, very quickly, our knowledge about what happens to man after he dies, fades out to the edge of uncertainty and then into the unknown.

And hear this: It is my conviction that the New Testament leaves a number of crucial questions unanswered.

The problem for us, then, is as to how far we feel that it is profitable to speculate.

Before I stop talking, I want to try to say to you with some mild dogmatism what I believe the New Testament teaches about those who are not Christian, and as to what happens to them when they die.

I say with just some small measure of dogmatism, I have here my senior thesis which I wrote at seminary. I make no claim for its scholarship other than that it is to this point. The title is

"Those Who Do Not See Life Eternal—a Discussion of the Doctrine of the Final Destiny of the Unregenerate" . . . which is a real impressive title. What it means is, it's dealing . . . this hundred pages deals with *every passage of Scripture,* that has anything to do with what happens to people when they die . . . those people who are not Christian. And every passage of Scripture is listed and dealt with.

Whereas there are many things about which I'm not dogmatic—and doubtless there is some poor scholarship in there—there has at least been one time in my life when I have tried to deal with this particular question in exhaustive detail.

And so I *shall* try to say to you what are my own convictions growing out of this, but I need to go at it once again from one more direction, in order to try to deal with this profitably.

Early in the life of the church—probably in the Apostolic era, certainly in the post-Apostolic days—once the Church had begun very clearly to preach Christ crucified and Christ resurrected, with the assurance of eternal life, with the concomitant assurance that God is a loving, forgiving, all-wise, all-powerful Heavenly Father, who offers eternal life through Christ Jesus . . . this Jesus who said, "I am the Way, the Truth, and the Life . . ."

Once this impact had come upon the church, and upon society, then four questions arose for which the Church had no answer:

What happens to babies who die in infancy?

What happened to all the people in the Old Testament—all the Old Testament heroes, Moses, and Abraham, and David, and all those people who never heard about Christ—what happened to them when they died?

What happens to all of the people outside of the Christian tradition who are obviously good people and living as best they know how, and who never even have a chance to accept Christ because they never hear about Him?

And finally, what is the fate of those who having heard the message of the Good News, reject Christ and refuse to accept Him as Lord and Savior?

The Church was confronted with these four problems. And I say to you that on this morning of nineteen hundred and sixty-two, the Church is *still* confronted with the problem of what to do with these four groups. Anyone who feels that he has a completely satisfactory answer to this enigma, has not tried to face with intellectual honesty the problems which surround it.

The Church, once confronted with this, got pretty frantic to try to find some way to deal with it. Searching around in the Scripture, they came across these two strange passages which we read and which seem to have something to do with the situation.

The Church, not knowing what happened to Christ from the time of His death to His Resurrection, assumed, and said, "Well, here's the answer: Christ went to wherever the dead are, and preached to people, and then was resurrected." And, many believed and concluded, that He went and preached to the people who had already died, and this gave them a second chance. He preached to all of the saints of the Old Testament, and gave them a chance to accept Him so that they could have eternal life.

If you find this helpful, if you find this interpretation something that resolves your problem, then this is the legitimate basis for putting into your own recitation of the Creed, *He descended into hell.*

And I say, sincerely, that it's right and proper as a Christian, that when we recite the Creed, that in your own inward recitation, you include the phrase, *He descended into hell,* which is certainly a part of our Christian tradition . . . no reason why you shouldn't do so.

As for myself, I'm glad that we leave it out, because I do not find the phrase helpful. I do not even find the interpretation of these two verses getting us much further, because, let us say . . .

(If at any point, I sound like I'm being facetious, I'm not. Sometimes my own corrupted mind makes me try to be smart-alecky when I really don't mean to be.)

But to my mind, we've still got a problem if we take care of those who died before Christ and give them another chance, and take care of the saints of the Old Testament, we're still stuck with the problem of what to do with babies who die in infancy, and what to do with those outside of our Christian tradition who never have a chance to hear about Christ. So I'd rather just deal with the whole problem head-on, than to solve it halfway with this phrase, *He descended into hell.*

I should like to try to present to you what I believe the New Testament teaches. And here's what I believe: Now in order that I may do this, I will need your cooperation and a little bit of mental discipline, in an effort to try to divest your mind of a number of pre-conceptions.

Let me make a little analogy here as to what I believe can take place. I can take a piece of iron—which is not particularly different from any other piece of iron—and wave it over wood, or glass, or paper, or cloth, and nothing happens. Take this same piece of iron, wave it over some iron filings, and immediately they *leap* to this iron because it's a magnet.

I believe that if we could divest our minds of a lot of preconceptions which are not Scriptural and which are not Christian, and let the New Testament speak to us directly, that there is some truth that with a new clarity would *leap* to our minds as the iron filings leap to the magnet.

Try this with me . . . try picturing yourself along the shore of the Sea of Galilee, and Jesus is teaching. And you and I are sitting and listening, and there are hundreds of other people. Jesus is not talking particularly about life after death, He's just doing some of his marvelous teaching. Suppose that as he's teaching, and we're listening, somebody should stop *Him* and say to *us,* "When you think of death, and what happens to a person when he dies, what comes to your mind?"

If some one should ask us there, in that setting, and ask the other people who were listening to Jesus, this is the kind of answer that one would get:

"Well, I believe that man is body and spirit—and they are real tightly tied together—and that when a man dies somehow or other his spirit still sort of needs his body, and so we ought to take care of the body. And I don't know what happens

54

to the spirit. It kind of floats around, I guess. Maybe there are a lot of spirits floating around; I don't know just what they do or where they are. Then maybe, somehow, when the body finally disintegrates, maybe the spirit just disappears too."

That would be about as far as any clarity of thinking went in the minds of those who were listening to Jesus. They would have heard some other speculation here or there, but this would be pretty much what was in their minds.

That leaves many, many questions unanswered, because it leaves many questions unasked. And I believe that when the Apostle Paul was writing, and when Jesus was speaking, that in *their* minds they were speaking and writing to *that* kind of a frame of reference. To bear this in mind would make quite a bit of difference in how one interprets what is in the Scripture.

It was after the preaching of the resurrection that death brought with it the sense of moral crisis, because now that through Christ, man is offered life eternal, this great gift from God, then one begins to wonder what happens to those who do not have this great gift. Rather quickly then, the Church divided between heaven and hell and then the pictures got to being drawn—some pretty wild pictures—drawn of the people who were down here, rather than up there.

If this is heresy, make the most of it:

I cannot believe, and do not believe, and will not believe, that God Almighty creates some human beings whom He knows when He creates them . . . when they die are going to a physical hell, or a hell of any kind. By this I mean physical only in the sense of having conscious reality . . . that people when they die, consciously go to some place of torture, however described, where they are tortured interminably through years and years and years on without end.

I do not believe that. And if one has to be Christian to believe that, then I'm not a Christian. As it so happens, I do *not* believe that is what Scripture teaches.

Now Jesus says more about what happens to people after death in terms of any punishment, than anybody else in the New

Testament. As a matter of fact, unless I'm mistaken, he's the only one. Because the Apostle Paul, for example, just only refers to life and death. I'll come back to that in a moment.

Jesus used the word—not hell—he used the word g-e-h-i-n-n-o-m, "gehinnom". And when he was speaking to these people here in Palestine, and said that the wicked would be cast into "gehinnom," a very physical picture came to their minds.

They thought about the Valley of Gehinnom outside of Jerusalem —some distance away—which was the refuse pile for the city. Remember there was no sanitation, there were no sewers, there was no garbage disposal, there was no way to dispose of the trash and the filth of the city. A good part of it got carried out here to this Valley—dead animals, garbage, and so on, were thrown out here. There was a constant fire burning . . . there was an unbearable stench . . . there was always the smoke going up . . . and no one went out there if he could possibly help it other than to leave his trash, his dead animals, and come back.

All right, now. Jesus was saying that the wicked, if they persist in their wickedness, would be thrown into the Valley of Gehinnom, and that was the picture that came to men's minds.

This was not an original idea with Jesus, he was only repeating what people recognized . . . that when the wicked die, they ought to be destroyed or be burned up . . . done away with. This was as far as Jesus' picture goes. And when we start going beyond that, we start going beyond what the Scripture has to say. As I say, the Apostle Paul just speaks of life and death. What do I believe?

I believe that if you will go to the New Testament and can find some way for it to speak to you without preconceptions, you'll come away with the overwhelming assurance that if you want life eternal, you may have it through Christ Jesus. You will come away with the assurance, that we cannot be dogmatic about anything else in the New Testament. But for myself, when I read the New Testament it leaves me with the feeling that if you are not Christian that when you die, you're dead . . . that's it.

Then for me, the New Testament speaks to that as being the answer. To me, I have the feeling that this is what the New Testament teaches.

56

And this would not be in any conflict with Jesus saying that the wicked shall be burned up . . . destroyed, because there's one other term that I want to use and close with: there is focal in the New Testament a conception which I am not sure was in the minds of those to whom Jesus spoke very much, because they were not speculating on this next thing.

But clearly in the teaching of John, and elsewhere, we have this idea of the eternal . . . that the eternal is time-less-ness, absence of time.

You see, long ago we recognized that heaven must be spaceless-ness. We don't think in terms of a spacial heaven, but if you'll pause a minute, you'll recognize without space you can't have time anyhow. But this is a genuine New Testament conception . . . timelessness.

Therefore, when you and I speak of moving out of this life into what lies beyond, we're not talking about moving into endless time, but into spacelessness and timelessness. So then, you see, if we are talking about eternal life, this is a life appropriate for the sphere of timelessness . . . eternity. Then if one must deal with eternal punishment—this does not mean endless punishment, it means punishment that is appropriate to eternity, and this we can leave to a loving God. It is my own conviction that the Scriptures point to the fact that within and beyond this punishment comes the end of those who have not come to God through our Lord Jesus Christ.

This is the end, this is all.

All right now . . . I speculated quite a bit as to whether or not I should even preach this sermon this morning because I know I've raised some questions that I have not answered.

I know this is a difficult area. I felt that you'd rather have me struggle with it, than to try to avoid it. The only reason I would avoid it is just because it's difficult to deal with . . . to make it have any clarity.

If I have raised questions which I have not answered, will you through a note, or through a telephone call, or in some fashion, let me know this week, and I shall try as effectively as I can to deal with whatever questions I have raised and have not answered . . . or that you have raised, and you feel like I might be able to answer.

And with that to say that I commit this to God Almighty as being an area in which we can be sure of His *love,* His *forgiveness,* and His *justice.*

With that, *I* can rest.

February 25, 1962

HE
ASCENDED
INTO HEAVEN

IN THAT I ATTENDED a little church-related college, we had in our freshman year a year of required Bible study. I'm glad of that—that is as it should be.

The second year was an elective, having to do with Christian history and belief, the first semester being that of history. And then we started out the second semester with Christian beliefs.

I did not much like the professor, but I was doing okay and was studying conscientiously and was making an "A", for which I was to be grateful a little bit later. One day in class he called on me, and said,

"Mr. Johnson, how long does it take a soul to get to heaven?"

I thought he was joking, and I smiled and said, "I don't know, a second or two I guess."

He said, "No, I'm serious, how long does it take a soul to get to heaven?" I assured him that I did not know and he proceeded thereafter with some mathematics he had worked out of how it takes some several hours for a soul to get to heaven.

That night I went to see him and told him I was dropping the course, and as I look back I feel I was a little bit sophomoric, but I'm still glad that I did it.

To me, that was the kind of ridiculous speculation which reflects discredit on Christianity.

Therefore, as we talk about heaven this morning and life after death I recognize that there is speculation which can be distasteful because of its arbitrariness and some of the overtones which might be carried.

I hope to avoid that.

I was reassured by the response which you folks gave to my sermon last week when I preached on *He descended into hell.* There was a little flurry of letters and telephone calls which I did deeply appreciate, in addition to the number of kind things that were said following the service, which reassures me in speaking on this other topic this morning.

In this setting, let me say briefly to any visitors that we are working our way through the Apostles' Creed . . . last Sunday preaching on *He descended into hell.* We omit that as Presbyterians, and some other branches of the Church now omit it, because
> we feel that it raises more questions, and answers less questions, than it can do good
>> because the Biblical support for it is very thin
>>> and because it was so late incorporated into the Apostles' Creed.

This morning, then, we are dealing with the phrase, *He ascended into heaven.* And in dealing with heaven, I know that I shall fail to cover certain aspects of the topic. But will you not recognize with me that we will also be dealing with life after death next week when we discuss the day of judgment, and again later on when we deal with the phrase, "I believe in the bodily resurrection." Time requires that I be a little bit selective as to what I try to cover today.

Discussion of heaven in mine and your day is almost non-existent.

In preparation for today I checked through quite a collection of sermons which I have in books of sermons, and then quite a few volumes of theology.

60

In the sermons, where a man would collect his sermons for a year, or where he would have a series of sermons, usually one encounters, characteristically, an Easter sermon. And in this Easter sermon, the sermon characteristically again, lines up the traditional arguments for belief in immortality. And that's it—no real reference to heaven.

In the theology books, right at the end there is always a short, high-sounding chapter which carefully avoids any reference at all to hell, one way or the other, and very little about heaven.

Why has there come this united vow of silence on the subject of heaven?

I think there are a little cluster of reasons, some of them valid and some of them invalid.

Recent generations have reacted against the interpretation of Christianity wherein it manifested itself as being preoccupied with the other world. There was a time when the whole focus of Christian preaching was aimed at helping people escape from the tortures of hell and arrive at the bliss of heaven.

Preachers would give half of a sermon to describing a deathbed scene, blow by blow, and word by word. The whole aim and focus of Christian living seemed to be able to die a nice, long, lingering death, wherein someone could make a number of very morbid and moving comments for the sake of future generations . . . about how angels were floating around in the room and the glories of heaven could be seen in the distance.

Well, what's wrong with such an approach?

The Christian conscience saw several things wrong and reacted with proper insight. For example, the Christian Church saw—the Christian people saw—that such an approach of preoccupation with heaven and hell made Christianity the support of injustice— that pie in the sky by and by, the offer of future assurance in order to tolerate present injustice, was often used deliberately by those in power to keep the masses assuaged. And Marx was right—was it Marx or Ingall, I don't remember, who coined the phrase of "religion being the opiate of the people" for it was so used in Russia to keep the Russian peasant down and content while the hierarchy of the Church and the nobles of the country rode roughshod over them.

I am afraid that has been true in a certain fashion in my own beloved Southland. In textile communities—such as that in which I was reared—the factory over and over again paid the salary of the minister that ministers to the church of the textile workers.

This was not nearly as noble as it looked. It did not require any gagging of the preacher—he could say anything he wanted to preach—and it was only just a matter of being a little discerning in selecting the preacher, and only asking several crucial questions, the main one being, "how did he feel about labor unions?" Then turning him loose, religion was made an opiate of the people.

Much more frequently and more fairly—and I say this because I was reared in the South—such an approach, where it existed, was for the most part unconscious. But it did lead in our middle class and in our upper middle class—which is pretty characteristic of the Presbyterian—to a complacency regarding any need for any social reform. It cut the vitality of moving out to change the social situation, because one was only preoccupied with getting to heaven.

Talk about heaven has died away under the impact of the emphasis of the social gospel . . . the recognition that Christ does have things to say about *this* life, and that Christ did come to redeem *this* life, both for the individual and for society.

And so this loss of a preoccupation with a heaven and hell in the Church has for the most part been good. The Christian conscience and concern changed in emphasis, so that heavenly promises faded in the background.

I think a second reason why our talk of heaven has died away is because this present life which you and I live here in these United States—even in the face of several wars—is so pleasant that heaven offers little hope of improvement.

I'll enlarge on that a little bit later.

But you and I, for the most part, feel like that even with all of our complaints we're perfectly willing for heaven to wait.

The third reason for this loss of heavenly conversation and reflection is the impact of our scientific orientation, which has been gathering strength as time has gone on. It's much harder to believe in heaven now than it was when heaven was a place up there, and earth was a place here, and hell was a place down there . . . and heaven was just beyond the stars. We cannot believe in heaven any more as physically located at a certain spot in the universe. So it's hard to make heaven have any reality.

And so out of these influences, now we're at the place where it's even poor taste to talk in a social situation or a social setting about heaven. One refers to it now kind of whimsically and apologetically and speculates about it in kind of an old-fashioned way. It's an old-fashioned topic.

Each Sunday morning when I get to church, my good friend, Bob McSwain—who is our resident caretaker—comes in and brings me a cup of coffee. Bob and I have a lot of things to share, including our agricultural heritage. So when he came in this morning I asked him if he had fed the chickens. He said that yeah, he had. And then he said, "You know, incidentally, I did churn some buttermilk recently." He had been back down in North Carolina. And he said, "While I was down there, here was some unpasteurized sour milk and I churned me some buttermilk."

As he talked about it, I could feel my mouth water. The idea . . . you know, the buttermilk with just the little flecks of butter in it? And so I was practically drooling.

Socially now, heavenly hope is sort of like homemade buttermilk —something that is a sort of warm memory—not too crucial, but no longer to be taken for very serious consideration because it's just not practical to try to bother with it.

So much for why we have ceased to speculate.

But, nevertheless, this is so true that now I speak of my experience as a minister. So far have we pushed speculation about heaven into the background that even when, as the minister, I find myself ministering to an individual or a family where there has been a recent death, I can say to you that rarely, if ever, does the question

63

come up in the conversation about the state and condition of the person who has now entered the gates of heaven. But, even though these questions are not asked, I know they're there, and that's the reason that I am preaching this sermon this morning.

If I may be a smarty pants for a moment, I hereby pass my own papal decree that it's good religion and good taste to speculate about the nature of heaven.

We may have very few answers, but we have the right to ask the questions, such as these: "How long does it"—no—I won't ask that.

But it is fair to ask, what can we legitimately know and try to envision about heaven? Is it naive or realistic to try to envision the state and condition of those who are in heaven?

Things such as this . . . is there recognition of loved ones in heaven?

What shall we do, specifically, about such matters as these and what should our thoughts be?

Do babies remain babies? Believe me, this is a question that comes to many people's minds and hearts.

People who die in their youth, do they remain youthful as far as whatever their attitude is in heaven?

What do people do with their time?

Well, after we have stopped making our smart cracks about playing on harps and sitting on clouds, actually, if one goes to heaven and one is self-aware, what does one actually do with his time . . . what are the activities?

What's the challenge of heaven?

Do our loved ones know what we are doing?

How can they be happy when they know how much pain there is in the world?

How about our beloved pets?

Maybe this is the place to raise the question about angels. Where do angels—which are many times mentioned in the Bible—where do they fit into this scheme of things? What's their relationship to heaven?

And then a bit more basically . . . how can we reconcile serious consideration of such matters in the face of this basic problem of a lost or surrendered conception of heaven as a physical location?

May I say to you that this *is* the basic problem that makes it awfully hard to deal with the matter of heaven and cuts the ground out from under speculation again and again.

In the face of these, how do we deal with the matter?

For whatever it may be worth to you, here's the way *I* deal with heaven.

First, I recognize with gratitude and admiration the unique—get this—the unique restraint of the New Testament in refusing to build these vast speculations regarding the nature of heaven. You only realize how grandly unique our New Testament is when your bother to read the religions of the world.

Really, only in the Book of Revelation is there speculation about the nature of heaven, and here this is consciously done for a specific purpose for the sake of those people who are now under persecution. It may well, indeed, have been written by John, the beloved apostle. If it were he who wrote the Book of Revelation, he would be *certainly* the one to recognize that he was dealing about heaven in an analagous fashion . . .

For it is John more than anyone else who reveals clearly that of which I was speaking last Sunday . . . that to move into the realm beyond death is to move into a timeless—not an endless time, but a timeless—era that eternality means "absence of time." So John—if it was he who wrote the Book of Revelation—would be constantly recognizing that he was accommodating the human mind to the sublime which lay ahead.

So that's the first thing that I'd do is to recognize that there is very little speculation in the New Testament regarding the nature of heaven.

65

Then, I remind myself that in trying to deal with the existence and relationships in heaven, I am dealing with an area in which space and time have no reality—or are not limiting factors, let me put it that way—and that therefore my own imagination breaks down in trying to deal with this.

That means that it is hard to envision heaven and it's harder to believe in heaven than it used to be. So it means then that I recognize, in the third place, that any thoughts I have on heaven at all have to be—if I may use the technical word here—accommodations.

I have to recognize that whatever I am thinking has to be some form of analogy—it cannot be taken quite literally, ever.

But let's be careful, now. Having said this, let's not throw the baby out at the bath. Because we don't know and because we have not experienced heaven, and because we do not now have the resources to experience heaven, does not mean that heaven is not real.

Let me use an illustration here which I have used in the past and will use again because to me it has a marvelous validity:

There is a young lady whom I know and whom I love who is to me a great person . . . a marvelously happy person . . . having only one limiting factor, and that is that she was born blind.

We need not waste any time feeling sorry for her because, as I say, she is a real happy, and adequate, and wonderful person. But many times I think, how would I answer if this little gal said to me, "Dr. Johnson, what do you mean by color—by red, and blue, and green?"

How would you answer a person who had never seen?

How would you describe color?

So, of course, all she can do is struggle for analogies.

But, because this little critter has never seen color, does that mean that there is no sunset?

Does that mean that these roses out here in the spring are not going to have any color?

66

Of course not.

It only means that for some reason, known only to God, she is minus the capacity at the moment to get this reality. But the reality is there.

So the same way about heaven.

The fact that now I cannot think in terms that are minus space and time does not mean that heaven is not real. So having reminded myself of these accommodations—and that my accommodations are somewhat less than literal—then I feel perfectly free to speculate.

For example, as I have said, publicly and privately—somewhat whimsically and somewhat seriously—I hope heaven is very much like the Chesapeake Bay and that God Almighty will give me my first assignment to sail on it for a million years.

And then give me another assignment for a week, and then put me back on the first assignment.

Going back to these questions which were raised earlier about the circumstances of what heaven is like and the activity and the relationship of people in heaven . . . and these questions I raised a little bit earlier . . .

I feel perfectly free, as I say, to think of them in earthly terms and to speculate in earthly terms and to make analogies in earthly terms, sharpening them up a little bit, and maybe sort of making them a little bit more vague just to kind of fit in with my sensibilities of what it must be like in heaven. But I do feel free to speculate in terms of earthly things.

Why? Because I have a great precedent—Jesus himself: "In my father's house are many mansions. If it were not so, I would have told you."

I do not think that Jesus thought that there were houses of various size on the hillsides of heaven: "I go to prepare a place for you." And I think our Lord Jesus knew exactly what sort of accommodation he was having to make when he spoke of the places in heaven.

Therefore, since our Lord Jesus spoke of heaven in earthly terms with marvelous and beautiful restraint, I feel perfectly free to do the same thing.

To ask finally . . . how much do I dream about and how much do I long for heaven?

Not much.

I can be even more honest than that—not *any*.

But when I do, I can make it take on a little glow if I take the greatest
    and the richest
        and the most rewarding
            and the most thrilling and challenging part of life
            and thrust it up into heaven.

If I can make it glow just a little bit in the light of a
    loving
        living
            crystal Christ
then truly and properly my heaven takes on a heavenly glow.

—March 4, 1962

THE
QUICK
AND
THE DEAD

Last Monday afternoon at 4:30 I left by car with a couple of friends to drive down to Richmond, and thereupon set out upon a night long to be remembered.

As I say, we left at 4:30 in the afternoon and arrived at the Hotel Jefferson in Richmond at 3 o'clock the next morning . . . ten and a half hours to go a hundred miles.

We had an excellent driver—not me—and we had a fine automobile—not mine. We had no particular difficulty with the car, and we were not stuck a single time. But there were several times when we sat for as much as one hour without moving a wheel. Why? Well, not as much on account of the snow, and the sleet, and the rain, and the slush as you might think. Primarily, because people were not obeying *one single law* . . . and that was of staying on the right side of the road.

Which leads one to ask, "Is there anything inherently wrong with driving on the left side of the road?" Well, there was *that* night! But now the truth of the matter is, and seriously, there is nothing wrong—and in England, as many of you know first hand, and as I know as a matter of general information—people drive regularly on the left hand side of the road. So the side that one drives on is perfectly arbitrary, and yet here in this nation we have a *law* . . . a law that says you must drive on the right hand side of the road. And we can even put people in *jail* for driving on the left hand side.

What does that have to do with the sermon? Well, it's a good point to raise a very difficult and searching question . . . "Who or what makes some things right and some things wrong?" Are there some things that are always everywhere, all of the time, always right, and are there some other things everywhere, all the time, always wrong . . . or is life made up of ordinances like which side of the road one will drive on? Rules that at long last are completely arbitrary . . . they're all right, they make life orderly, and we ought to obey them. But it would be just as well if they were turned exactly the other way around. If you have given this any thought, previously—or if you have read on it at all—you realize that we are dealing with one of the most profound aspects of human life. That is the problem of ethics . . . of morality . . . of whence cometh right and wrong.

What do we mean by good and evil?

Is there any ultimate good and evil?

I might say in passing that there are many Christians who feel—and I think that I must put myself in this category—that there is a real sense in which we are trapped with a kind of ultimate moral relativism . . . that there is good, there is evil, there's the right and the wrong. But somehow or other, we're always struggling to find out just exactly what it is.

There are other people wtih greater minds than my own who are committed to a moral finality . . . a moral specificity . . . that these things are right and these things are wrong, always and at all times.

Be that as it may, this thing of what is right and what is wrong is much more complex and much more difficult than appears on the surface.

Let me tell you something that I have been turning over in my own mind during this past couple of weeks—as a matter of fact I've done it on many occasions—asking myself this about myself . . . How much of my conduct—thinking principally now of my

70

moral conduct—how much of my conduct is controlled by fear? More specifically, fear of punishment . . . punishment from society —that is, from man—or punishment from God.

And ask along in the same frame of reference . . . How much *should* I be controlled by fear?

How legitimate is fear of punishment as a device for controlling me and other people?

Man's punishment or God's punishment? This is a better topic for discussion than you realize, and when you get around the dinner table, you start chewing this over, and you'll find out that this is a very probing aspect of life.

I never have been abroad to witness this firsthand, but I assume that it is true, this thing that we hear about the conduct of the so-called "ugly Americans." Not infrequently, many Americans are terribly embarrassed by the misconduct of their fellow Americans as soon as they get abroad.

Why do these people, as soon as they get away from home, start acting like this? Is it because they are out from under the restraint of the fear of punishment? Specifically, the punishment of social rejection which they would have at home?

How would I act, and I'm moving into another little phase now, and moving down a bit closer to our central theme . . . how would I act if I were convinced that there were no God? Or—what is the same thing—if I were convinced that God Almighty neither knows nor cares about what goes on in the affairs of mankind . . . that God makes no judgments regarding good and evil . . . what difference would this make in my conduct?

I've recently read a little book entitled, *In the Midst of Life*. If I recall correctly, the author's name is Bates, and this is the record of a man's reflections as he faces certain death. For this man went to his physician, and discovered that he had an inoperable tumor, and that therefore he had a year to a year and a half to live with this malignancy, which was certain to take his life.

And so this man who was already an author, began to write down his reflections and his feelings about this thing that lay ahead of him, this mystery of death. This was a man who was an atheist, and for whom his atheism was fairly important. And he voiced this atheism over and over again in the book. Yet, as one reads it, he discovers that this man, in his early life, had lived a rather conventional life, neither particularly good nor bad, and that facing death his life remained somewhat in the same conventional pattern. So that somehow or other this matter of God or no God didn't seem to have had much effect one way or the other.

On the other hand, I have read this little review in *Time* magazine this week about the great playwright Tennessee Williams, who also, if I read the story correctly as we read about him and about his plays, manages to convey to me through this interview, his conviction that beyond this life in which we live, there is nothing. Therefore we better get out of this life what we can. And if one is to read between the lines, one assumes that Mr. Williams and his characters are determined so to do.

How would you act if you were convinced that there is no God? You can't say for sure, and neither can I, but I'm challenging you this morning, when you get home, to reflect on it a bit.

For those of you who are here for the first time, we are in the midst of a series of sermons on the Apostles' Creed. We come this morning to the phrase. *He sitteth on the right hand of God the Father Almighty; from thence He shall come to judge the quick and the dead.*

Last Sunday, we spoke on the phrase *He ascended into heaven* and may I remind you that we will be dealing with some other aspects of eternal life and of life after death when we come to the phrase *I believe in the resurrection of the body and the life everlasting* which we shall do on Easter Sunday.

Now, one other parenthesis, this phrase that I just quoted, *He sitteth on the right hand of God the Father Almighty*—when you think about it, you'll realize that this brings primarily to mind the problem of the Trinity. Therefore, rather than dealing with that phrase this morning, I should like to set it on the side, because next Sunday morning we shall be dealing with the phrase *I believe in the Holy Ghost* which brings us face to face with this topic. Let us come now to the phrase, *He shall come to judge the quick and the dead.*

Of course, this word "quick" is the old Anglo-Saxon word which just means "alive." As this phrase is meant to do . . . as it does, whenever we recite it, *He shall come to judge the quick and the dead* . . . it brings up the scene of the last judgment as we read it here in Matthew . . . the final day of the world when the judge of the world sits and passes judgment on the moral conduct of mankind.

I'd like for you to notice several things about this phrase. In the first place—along with whatever problems it may bring—it points out that *Christ* is to be the judge of the world. This is Scriptural as we read both in Matthew and over in the Book of Revelation, that strange passage over there.

So this at least calls our attention to a mistake that you and I make intellectually and I think emotionally over and over again in our Christian theology. It comes about from our not pushing our own Christian conceptions to the point where they should go. You and I far too many times get preoccupied with Christ as the Redeemer of mankind, as we should—with His life, death, and resurrection—and of what He has done for us through this.

I want to say something now that may sound sacrilegious. I don't mean it to be sacrilegious at all, so please don't take it whimsically or sacrilegiously, but to try to make a point:

Far too many times you and I think of God Almighty as being the bad guy, and that Christ is the good guy who comes along and saves us from the bad guy. We forget that the Scripture says *God* so loved the world that *He* gave His only begotten son. This is God's act, and over and over again, our Lord Jesus says the very purpose for His coming is to demonstrate God as loving, forgiving, heavenly Father. This is what characterizes Him. So at least this phrase—*He shall come to judge the quick and the dead*—puts Christ in the role of the judge, and at least makes us

> refocus
>> and reevaluate
>> and reestablish

our relationship between our Heavenly Father, and ourselves, and our Lord Jesus Christ.

This picture of the judgment day—as soon as you start thinking about it—brings such a welter of intellectual problems. They come flowing in so fast as to make one wonder where to start in dealing with the judgment day.

I hope that I've proven in this series by now that I'm not out to duck any problems of any kind . . . the very purpose of preaching this series is to deal with the problems. If I have done that, may I then have the privilege of pointing out first, the positive value of this concept . . . what we seize onto and hold onto as of value in this conception of the judgment day . . . and then if there're problems we'll try to deal with them with what time we have.

Christ shall come to judge the quick and the dead.

This takes us directly back to the problem with which we opened this sermon, and that is the problem of the *source* of moral judgments. Who says, or what says, or where do we get the idea of right and wrong, of good and evil? And this phrase . . . every time we recite the Apostles' Creed . . . this phrase, *He shall come to judge the quick and the dead,* brings us face to face with this fact:

That *God*—hear me now—that *God Almighty,* and He alone, determines good and evil. Good is what God wills . . . this is good. Evil is what is contrary to the will of God. Therefore, that which is evil—or that which partakes of evil—must at some point stand under God's divine judgment.

You and I as human beings may have a lot of trouble finding out what God's will is. I say this with some reservation—but it's pretty much my conviction—that I question whether there is *ever* a time in life when we can be absolutely, unqualifiedly, dogmatically certain that we know God's will. But we know this: that wherever we do find God's will, *that is the good.* And the evil then, is that which is contrary to the will of God.

So that's where good and evil come from. And this phrase—whenever we recite it in the Creed—says that God Almighty does not overlook or forget about evil. He passes judgment on it. This is something that we need constantly to put into our corrective picture of God Almighty, lest we in our day and time turn God into a gentle, senile, dottering, old grandfather.

74

God is not a dottering, old grandfather. God is *God*.

God is *love*. And in our recognition that God is *love,* it behooves us to recognize that God is also *justice*. I don't think we can have a God of love without a God of justice, because to lose the concept of justice is to end up with a God who just doesn't care.

I have to say to you in all honesty that I'm not at all concerned this morning about what any specific boys are doing in New York City or in Paris, other than as a human being I would like for all boys to be good everywhere, or something like that, and I have a concern for humanity. But in reality, I could not care less, because I don't even know them. Therefore, when I lose my moral concern for them, I also lose my love for them. By the same token, whenever we lose our conception of God Almighty as a God of justice, we are just that moment before losing our God of love.

You think about that.

God's moral judgment may raise and does raise many problems which I cannot settle . . . raises them for me. But in this old difficult world in which we live, I find it tremendously reassuring—not threatening, but tremendously reasssuring—that to God Almighty good and evil *do* matter, and that what I do makes a difference right on out to the fringes of eternity.

Letting that sit for a moment, let me try to deal with a little bit of the cluster of problems that surround this day of judgment. I guess this is sort of the basic problem for us as twentieth century Christians:
> When is the day of judgment?
> > And where is the day of judgment?
> > > And what happens to people who die between now and judgment day?

At the risk of being repetitious, let me remind you that, as far as I'm concerned, when we are dealing with the idea or the concept of that which lies beyond death—in the realm of the eternal—we are always doing this (and I want to use a word that I used last Sunday, a technical word): we must always recognize that we are *accommodating,* and that is that we're using ideas which don't quite fit—no matter what ideas we use, and that they must be taken always as something less than literal.

This does not mean that they are not in a real sense true, but they cannot be taken with literalness. When we move out of this earth . . . when we move out of this world . . . I'm convinced that we move into a sphere where neither space nor time have any meaning. You and I can't think without these space-time concepts, and therefore always we have to build our little pictures. These pictures are helpful, but they're still pictures.

Therefore, for me—and this may or may not be of any help to you—when I think about the day of judgment, I constantly remind myself of this discontinuity between time and eternity which I cannot envision. For me then, the day of judgment is continuous. It has always been, is now, and so far as I can conceive, always will be.

The day of judgment is that which *always* is.

But I say to you, you must draw the picture with which you can live most comfortably and most rewardingly.

So this phrase, then, makes us face up again to the fact that God Almighty is the determiner of good and evil. But it also brings in this problem:

He shall come to judge the quick and the dead brings us to face once again our doctrine regarding the return of our Lord Jesus Christ.

I know I'm repeating myself here, but I must do so to round out this sermon.

You and I as Presbyterians, and I believe as Christians, are committed to the fact that our Lord Jesus Christ *will* return.

Sometimes we allow the sensational fringe of the Church to take this doctrine away from us and do with it such distorted things that we disclaim it, as for example . . . using it as a tool to bludgeon people over the head to try to do something about their fate now because our Lord Jesus Christ is destined to come over on Pennsylvania Avenue tomorrow afternoon at two o'clock.

76

I reject this. I remember that our Lord Jesus said that His return was the *one* thing that *only* the Father knew . . . that even Christ himself didn't know when He would return.

What does the return of Christ mean to me?

It means that at the *ultimate end of human history*—whatever that is—Christ will be there. Therefore, human history has a goal, a direction . . . that is, being shot like an arrow towards a goal. And, therefore, human history is not this endless cycle that goes on and on, so that human affairs make no difference. We are being thrust by human history down towards the goal that God Almighty has established, and at the end of that goal stands our Lord Jesus Christ.

That's what the return of Christ means to me.

I would like to say—because I think that you still encounter this sometimes in contemporary thinking—that several wars have made us quite more realistic in our conception of what we mean by the return of Christ, and what we mean by human history.

Before the first World War—for a generation or so—there was the naive feeling that humanity was on the glory road, and that here was a long slant right up towards glory and that humanity was marching happily along. And if it'd just keep on marching, it would march straight into heaven.

Then there came along one war, and that shook the world a little bit, made them realize that we were not marching straight to heaven. Then comes along another world war, and this naivete now has about disappeared.

Theologians, and other Christians, now recognize that the world can get better and worse at the same time, and probably does. So we're getting better and better and worse and worse, all at once.

Therefore, the end of human history rests not in man's hands, but in the hands of God. And God brings it when He is ready.

This is what we mean by the return of Christ, and to me—rather than being a threatening idea—this is tremendously reassuring . . . that human history is in God's hands.

Finally, I kept thinking about the judgment day some few months back—I tell you this because this sort of conveys the overtones of judgment day for me—when there was a little man, rather innocuous looking, who sat in a bullet-proof glass cage, over in Israel, while day after day the horrible enormities were paraded before mankind until we were all sick at the stomach again.

What man can do to man!

You see such enormous crimes, that finally there is no adequate penalty, and there is no place to put the blame. And there is no way to put the blame.

If I were a Jew, I don't know what my thoughts would have been. I don't know whether I would feel this same way, so I disavow my right to judge in part.

But I should like to think that even if I were a Jew in this particular circumstance, I would have been able to feel this way: that after all of these enormities had been paraded, and this little innocuous man sat there in his glass cage, and the judgment had been passed, and now the penalty was to be voiced, that the judge on the bench would quote those great words from the Old Testament . . . " 'Vengeance is *Mine. I* will repay, saith the Lord.' . . and until God Almighty pays, you shall serve the remainder of your life in prison."

And place judgment where it is meant to be, in the lap of God.

He shall come to judge the quick and the dead.

And I'm glad that the judgment of man is in the hands of God.

March 11, 1962

I BELIEVE
IN THE
HOLY GHOST

I F THERE WERE NOT some sort of inescapable and irreplaceable truth in the doctrine of the Trinity, I'm sure it would have been done away with long ago, for it is such a difficult doctrine . . . that we should know and worship God as one God, yet in three persons, Father, Son, and Holy Spirit.

This doctrine of the Trinity is, in my own experience, the one Christian doctrine which appears more confusing and untenable the more you think about it. As I have wrestled with it again—looking to this morning—and have sought to read back through the history of theology, I find that my wrestling and my reflections many times bring confusion rather than clarity.

How one should think about the relationship between the Father and the Son and the Holy Spirit—indeed, how one should even speak about it—was the very cause of the break between the Eastern and the Western branches of the Church. Those of you who were at the church night dinner recently remember that we had representatives speaking to us from the three branches of the Church—the Protestant, the Roman Catholic, and the Greek Orthodox.

And you remember that in the course of the discussion, Father Kalaris, of the Greek Orthodox Church, made some reference to the filioque clause or phrase in the Creed as having been the reason, externally, for the break between the Eastern and the Western branches of the Christian Church. And, then, Father Kalaris—at a request from those present—sought to clarify what he meant by the filioque phrase.

I'm afraid that with all good intentions he confused, rather than clarified, so now it's my turn to confuse.

Filioque is the Latin phrase which means "and from the son." Filio is the Latin word for son, and que, and. You remember from Aeneid, arma virumque cano, "of arms and the man I sing," so the *and* there—filioque is reversed, it means *and the son*.

So now to see where this phrase came in and broke up the Church. Since this does have to do directly with the doctrine of the Holy Spirit, let me go back now and repeat something I've repeated on some other occasions. That is, about the year 300 A.D., Constantine—who was the Emperor of Rome—became a Christian, and when he became a Christian, then overnight Christianity ceased being a source of persecution, and became suddenly respectable . . . politically and socially desirable.

This sudden success, or acceptance, which came to Christianity brought with it a rapid corruption, not unlike that which we encounter ideationally in some of the new African countries where being suddenly emancipated, whereas up until now the struggle has been for some form of survival, there has never been an opportunity for leaders to strengthen themselves so that they may prepare themselves, and thus lead in the new freedom.

This happened in the Church in similar fashion. After all, everybody was fighting to survive down in the catacombs and all of a sudden the Church is free and accepted, and the leadership has not been stabilized in such a fashion as to stabilize the Church.

So there came some rather rapid corruption.

But there also came some good and proper things out of this period, for the Church came up out of the catacombs, looked around and caught its breath, and then said, "Now let's get together and find out what we really believe."

The Church began drawing up what we call the Ecumenical Creeds . . . the creed of the whole Church. And one of the first—and therefore one of the oldest—is what we call the Apostles' Creed. This is the Creed around which we are building this series of sermons, and come this morning to the phrase . . . *I believe in the Holy Ghost.*

After the Apostles' Creed was adopted by the Church, and the theologians began going back and working through it, they realized that there were some things that needed to be spelled out that had not been made clear in the Creed. For example, though the Creed spoke of Christ and of His being the Son of God, it did not clarify the *relationship* between Christ and the Father.

And so the Church launched out on its first great theological controversy. It had to do with a Greek word, *homoousion,* as over against another Greek word, *homoiousion,* the only difference being a little *iota,* a little Greek letter which was probably the biggest controversy over the littlest letter in the history of Christendom. But this was not just arguing over spelling, for the two words mean *same* substance and *like* substance.

This was the battle to say whether Christ was the same as the Father or like substance with the Father. Involved in this— which seems to be of no consequence—was the critical question as to whether or not Christ was fully divine.

We may have our own difficulties with the doctrine of the divinity of Christ, but I think there is no question, historically, that if the divinity of Christ had not been fully established, then Christianity would have died. So, the homoousians won and the full divinity of Christ was established.

Then the church set out on another theological controversy. This one went on for several hundred years . . . on down until it got to be ultimately crystalized in the eighth century.

By this time the controversy was between the Eastern branch of the Church and the Western, and the Eastern branch and the Western branch had become theologically somewhat differently oriented. They were socially differently oriented between Constantinople and Rome, politically different in their orientation, so that in reality there actually were now two branches of the Church that were just waiting for a good issue on which to crack in two.

Incidentally, now we are talking about a break in our Church, because this was the only Church there was. So now here comes the argument on which the Church finally broke in two, and if this seems to confuse you,
     it's not because you are stupid,
          it's not because you're not theologically oriented,
               it's not because you are not listening carefully
. . . it's because it's confusing.

In the several hundred years since this first controversy, the argument was going on about the Holy Spirit, and what to do with the Holy Spirit. And everybody agreed that the Father had not *created* the Holy Spirit.

This wouldn't work, so somebody said, "Well, then, how *is* the Holy Spirit related to the Father?" . . . and some wise guy came up with a real high sounding phrase.

He said . . . "The Son proceeds eternally from the Father."

What does that mean? I don't know, but it sounds real good and it looked like it was going to settle the argument.

All right.

The Eastern branch of the church said this is a good phrase. The Father is the source of all power and all truth, so, of course, the Holy Spirit *also* proceeds eternally from the Father.

The Western Church said . . . "Oh, no, hold off here. You have forgotten that we've already had a controversy in which we have established the fact that the Son is of the *same* substance with the Father and therefore the Holy Spirit proceeds from the Father and the Son . . . filioque, from the Father *and the Son.*

The Eastern Church said . . . "No, this is wrong."

And the Western Church said . . . "Yes, this is right."

So when the Western Church wrote their next creed, they put in the filioque clause—or the filioque phrase—and the Son . . . that the Holy Spirit proceeds from the Father and the Son.

82

So, you and I now find ourselves pounding our heads in frustration, saying . . . "I don't know what they were saying, I don't know what that phrase means, and I do not see how it could possibly make any difference in the Church and in the well-being of the Kingdom of Christ."

I'm very much inclined to agree. But before I do, let me say several things about this controversy which must be said.

Somehow, and somewhere, in the history of the Church it was absolutely necessary that the finest minds of the Church, the theologians, sit down and wrestle through together every aspect of Christian theology. Christianity was destined—as it is destined today—to be encountered by the best intellects of the pagan world, as it should be. The Christian Church had to be ready to wrestle out with the pagan world—the best in the pagan world, the intellectually best—every aspect of Christian theology.

And we'd better be glad that the Church did take its best minds and do this.

In the second place, these controversies raged as they did because the best minds in the world—certainly the best minds in the Western world—were dedicated to the Church . . . minds which today would be given many times to science, to politics, other things. But the Church had the best minds of the day.

Let it be said further that I am convinced—and I think there is plenty of evidence to point out or to support this—that whereas we know more—we have more facts in our day—we're not inherently any more brilliant as human beings than any other previous generation.

For example, I think we could go back 4,000 years to Abraham and to Moses and to some of these great men and bring them down into our day and they'd still be great, outstanding men. The Church had minds which would be comparable with the best minds of our day wrestling with their theology.

I want to say something here in parentheses which has nothing to do with the topic, but it needs to be said and I want to say it.

The Church of Jesus Christ needs in this generation, in the next generation, and the generation after that—still needs and will desperately need— the finest minds of the world.

I want to talk to you youngsters, out here and up there in the balcony, as I spoke to the youngsters at the 9:30 service.

I want to challenge you in the name of our Lord Jesus Christ to think about, and pray about, whether it may not be that God Almighty wants you to give your life to full time service of the Church of our Lord Jesus Christ . . . as a minister, or as a missionary, or as a director of Christian education, or in some other sphere . . . full time dedication to the Church of Christ. Our nation has recently challenged its young people to dedicate themselves to our Peace Corps. I challenge you to become a part of the Peace Corps of our Lord Jesus Christ.

I have given my life and am giving my life to this, and therefore I can bear personal testimony to the fact that
    it can be terribly discouraging
        it can be heartbreaking
           it can be wearying.

But it can be so tremendously exhilarating and rewarding and deeply satisfying regarding the ultimate purposes of life that I say to you that in my own opinion, and from my own experience, it's still the greatest calling in the world.

You go home and pray about it and think about it and see if God Almighty wants you to take your mind, and your heart, and your life and give them to the Church of our Lord Jesus Christ.

Back to something that may be less thrilling than making that statement, but it is something that all of us need to wrestle with. Back to this question of what do we do with this talk about the Holy Spirit.

What do we believe and think about the Holy Ghost?

The Church had to wrestle with it because the Church believed in the Holy Spirit, and therefore the Church had to say something about Him, or It—preferably Him—for we should use the pronoun here. To use a pat parlance phrase of the street of several years ago, "Here is my problem, Mr. Anthony."

Whenever I say—and I'm speaking for myself now—whenever I say . . . *I believe in the Father, the Son, and the Holy Spirit* . . . and when I reflect on it, it makes me have the feeling that I'm supposed to believe in three Gods . . . that I am a tritheist, if you please.

For me, having some theologian constantly whispering in my ear . . . "There is but one God in three persons, Father, Son, and Holy Spirit, but only one God" . . . this doesn't help me very much.

Let me assure you that my problem has been the problem right back to the time of Constantine. Just as soon as the Christian world started proclaiming its commitment to the Trinity—to the Father, the Son, and the Holy Spirit—the pagan world started saying . . . "Where are you any better than previous generations? You're nothing in the world but polytheists. You believe in three Gods . . . might as well believe in thirty."

The Church said . . . "Oh, no, we believe in only one God . . . in three persons." And the pagan world very properly said . . . "Have it your own way, make it easy on yourself . . . now explain it to us."

So the Church set about trying to explain it. Some fine mind quite sincerely would go off somewhere and think, and pray, and worry, and fret, and come up with some explanation as to how the Father, the Son, and the Holy Spirit were related to each other.

The Church council would meet, and would listen, and then would give his explanation a name, and then would declare this explanation inadequate, and then would say that it was heresy, and then would condemn the poor guy who thought it up, and then send somebody else out to make his try.

The series of heresies were named, such as
 Monarchianism
  and Doceticism
   and Modalism
    and Patripassianism
and so forth and so on.

I'm quite serious when I say to you . . . you may resolve this problem any way that you please. After you've worked it out in your own mind, go back and read Church history and you'll find out that the Church has already condemned that as heresy.

All right, what do we Presbyterians do about it?

I'm going to read to you what we Presbyterians believe about the doctrine of the Trinity . . . the Father, the Son, and the Holy Spirit. Here it is in this book, *The Confession of Faith,* which was drawn up by our forebears at the Westminster Assembly in Westminster Abbey several hundred years ago and handed down to us. This is our statement of our belief three times.

First, there's a statement of our profession of faith and our doctrine, and then it's put in catechetical form called the *Larger Catechism.* Then it's put in briefer form in the *Shorter Catechism.*

These are the four questions from the Larger Catechism having to do with the Trinity.

Question 8. *Are there more Gods than one?*

Answer: *There is but one only, the living and true God.*

That's simple.

How many persons are there in the Godhead?

There be three persons in the Godhead, the Father, the Son and the Holy Ghost; and these three are one, true eternal God, the same in substance, equal in power and glory, although distinguished by their personal properties.

Now that resolves it all, doesn't it? No problems.

What are the personal properties of the three persons in the Godhead? It is proper to the Father to beget the Son and to the Son to be begotten of the Father, and to the Holy Ghost to proceed from the Father and the Son—see, we're filioque—*from all eternity.*

How doth it appear that the Son and the Holy Ghost are God equal with the Father?

Question 11 gives the answer. *The Scriptures manifest that the Son and the Holy Ghost are God equal with the Father, ascribing unto them such names, attributes, works and worship as are proper to God only.*

86

If you have any more trouble with the doctrine of the Trinity, its your fault!

Really now, why does the Church still hold on to this difficult doctrine of the Trinity, and especially demand that it be stated in this difficult way?

Well, I don't know entirely, but I know part of the answer . . . and that is, that any doctrine or belief of the Church that keeps having vitality has that vitality, not because the Church says it should have, but because it keeps finding reality in the lives of Christians. I'm convinced that there's something about this Trinitarian conception of God including the Holy Spirit that keeps finding vitality and reality in the life of the Christian. Somehow or other, Christians have the kind of experience which could not be exhausted by talking about the Father and the Son. It has to do generally with the power of God in the world, as God is present and active in human affairs and in individual human lives.

Let me give you three classic examples from the Scripture of instances in which we seem to see this aspect of God appearing in human affairs in such fashion as to say, we must speak of the Holy Spirit. We read one for our selected reading today, when here were Christ's apostles and early disciples gathered together in a room, waiting for something to happen in their lives.

They believed in God, the Father of our Lord Jesus Christ, as their Heavenly Father. They believed in the risen Lord, who was now to be proclaimed by them. And then all of a sudden they felt surging through their lives this tremendous sense of power that thrust them out into the world, proclaiming the Gospel with such dynamic force that the world seized upon this new truth. They said . . . "This is because the Holy Spirit is moving in our lives."

When our Lord Jesus was baptized, he spoke, of course, of the Father. And then the Scriptures tell us that somehow or other there moved in Christ's life—as a dove descending—the power of the Spirit, so that now Christ was empowered to go out and in his public ministry do that which he was not empowered to do previously.

87

And then, finally, going back to the Old Testament . . . and incidentally, if you want to see this pictorialized, on this pulpit in two panels here are replicas of the coat of arms of the Southern Presbyterian Church, and if you'll come up and look at them you'll find among the other emblems there's a little bush and this is the burning bush which we have in the Old Testament when Moses was stopped in his tracks and was spoken to by God.

This was one of the great moments in human history when God empowered through His Spirit this man Moses to go out and with a new power move among the people of Israel to bring about God's purpose.

Somehow, when this kind of thing happens, we haven't resolved the matter enough when we speak of God the Father and God the Son. We must still speak in some sense of God the Spirit.

In closing, let me try to say to you how the matter of the Holy Spirit sits in my mind.

If you're interested in getting me burned at the stake, make a few notes from here on out and refer them to the authorities, because I will be talking pure heresy. People have been burned at the stake for the kinds of things I'm going to say. So if you're interested in some diversion in life, just take some notes.

I swing in my own thinking back and forth between being a polytheist; that is, believing in a multiplicity of Gods, on the one hand, and on the other extreme I find myself, from time to time, being a modalist; that is, believing that God appeared in several manifestations.

This has been condemned as heresy by the Church.

That first God appeared as the creator, and then God appears as the Son, and then God appears as the Holy Spirit. These three don't really remain as individual persons . . . this is just different manifestations of the same person.

So I get on down really to my heresy. I guess that I'm a bitheist in my thinking (if there is such a word), because I think, like the Creed, of God the Father Almighty, and the Son sitting on his right hand. I think of two people as running the universe, and, for me, the Holy Spirit, as such, doesn't have a person or personality. Therefore—though I know I should do it, because this is what the book says—I have a hard time referring to the Holy Spirit as "He." And for me to speak—as doubtless I should speak—of having a love for the Holy Spirit as a person has no reality for me.

Perhaps it should . . . perhaps this is my own theological inadequacy.

But I just thought that you might like to join me in this heresy. I don't want to get burned alone, so if there are any of you who care to join me, just let me know.

Does this disturb me . . . that I rock back and forth and have these confused ideas?

No, it really doesn't.

This thing is not resolved for us in Scripture, I guess, because it can't be. What is not clear in the Scripture is not going to keep me awake if it's not clear in my mind.

I do know this much. I do know that the God of the universe—whom I know to be its creator—has manifested Himself in Christ Jesus in such a way that through Him I can see God as a loving, Heavenly Father. By the same token, in this church, in my experience and in my own personal life, I have felt the Spirit of God move with power. Therefore—though I get all these confused, ridiculous ideas and nothing remains very clear many times —I do know that there is a validity, and there is a propriety, and there is a sincerity in my saying, like this over you many times at the close of a service . . .

"And now may the grace of our Lord Jesus Christ and the love of God and the fellowship of the Holy Spirit rest and abide upon you . . ."

because somehow or other the Spirit of God is in this church . . . and in thus fashion I do believe in God the Holy Spirit.

God the Father, God the Son, and *God the Holy Spirit.*

March 18, 1962

THE
HOLY
CATHOLIC
CHURCH

THE MOST BASIC RULE for proper Biblical interpretation is this: one must always interpret the Bible by the Bible or—as the theologian usually says it—Scripture must be interpreted by Scripture.

All sorts, of errors, and distortions, and misinterpretations have come about by some person searching around in the Scripture and finding some little isolated verse that happens, out of context, to appeal to his interpretation of life, and using this as that upon which to build some moral or theological superstructure.

In order to interpret the Scripture, we must bring all of the Scripture into focus, and let the Scripture bring about its own interpretation.

In the Apostles' Creed we say . . . *I believe in the holy catholic church*. In order to proclaim what I believe about the Church, it is necessary for me to consider the total teaching of the Scripture. Therefore, it is only as one stands in full before the total teaching of the Bible about the Church that he can come to know what the Church is meant to be.

Speaking of Scripture, the word "catholic" is not in the Bible. However, it is a good word; it's made up of two Greek words, κατα and ολος. *Cata* means according to or concerning, and *holos*

90

means just what it says, the whole thing. So, cata holos, from which comes "catholic," means concerning the whole matter, hence, worldwide or universal.

And the word "catholic" immediately brings to mind the Roman branch of the Catholic Church.

In this sermon this morning I should like to ask you to accord to me what I should like to think is basically a Christian spirit. That is, that here or there I should like to make analogies and contrasts between Protestant catholicism and Roman catholicism, as far as the conception of the Church is concerned.

I do not mean for these comparisons or these criticisms to be angry, or ugly, in any sense at all, but rather to try to make them factual, and where they're judgmental, that they should be fairly judgmental.

In this series, I have struggled as best I know how to be intellectually honest, and to try to make this series of sermons on the Apostles' Creed instructive and informative. I have no desire at all to be contentious, but by the same token God grant that I should not be mealy-mouthed.

So let me try to say the things that I think pertain to this matter, having first spoken of my common love, or my love for all of those who share with me our common love for our Lord Jesus Christ.

To try to demonstrate the spirit in which I would do this, let me be critical, if I must, of two of our denominations at the same time—put them in the same frame of reference—the Roman branch of the Church, and the Disciples of Christ branch of the Church. I do find myself resisting allowing my brethren of the Roman branch of the Church to take over the word "catholic." That's my word, too.

Therefore, I think it's just confusing to talk about Catholics.

I'm a catholic.

I'm a Presbyterian catholic.
    There *are* Presbyterian catholics
        and Roman catholics
            and Baptist catholics.

91

That sounds strange doesn't it?

I have an uncomfortable feeling about our brethren of the church of the Disciples of Christ, calling their church the "Christian Church". Somehow or other, that makes for so much confusion in verbiage because—however misled I may be—I think of us Presbyterians as being Christians. It just confuses the issue for the Disciples to call their church the Christian Church . . . as it is confusing for our Roman brethren to call their church the Catholic Church.

I believe in the holy catholic church.

I'd like to read to you two passages out of the Scriptures, and the reason I'm reading them is because they're the *only* two places in the Bible where our Lord Jesus makes any reference to the Church. He only uses the word "Church" twice. There's a framework of about five verses in each instance, and so I should like to read them to you.

One of them is from the 16th chapter of Matthew, the other from Matthew 18.

"Now when Jesus came into the district of Caesarea Philippi, he asked his disciples 'Who do men say that the Son of man is?' And they said, 'Some say John the Baptist, others say Elijah, and others Jeremiah or one of the prophets.' He said to them, 'But who do you say that I am?' Simon Peter replied, 'You are the Christ, the Son of the living God.' And Jesus answered him, 'Blessed are you Simon Bar-jona! For flesh and blood has not revealed this to you, but my Father who is in heaven. And I tell you, you are Peter, and on this rock I will build my church, and the powers of death shall not prevail against it. I will give you the keys of the kingdom of heaven, and whatever you bind on earth shall be bound in heaven, and whatever you loose on earth shall be loosed in heaven.' Then he strictly charged the disciples to tell no one that he was the Christ."

Then over to the 18th chapter, verse 15, and Jesus is still speaking, and now he's speaking to all of the disciples. He says, "If your brother sins against you, go and tell him his fault, between you and him alone. If he listens to you, you have gained your brother. But if he does not listen, take one or two others along with you, that every word may be confirmed by the evidence of two or three witnesses. If he refuses to listen to them, tell it to the church; (And here's his other instance of the use of the word "church.") and if he refuses to listen even to the church, let him be to you as a Gentile and a tax collector. Truly, I say to you, whatever you bind on earth shall be bound in heaven, and whatever you loose on earth shall be loosed in heaven. Again I say to you, if two of you agree on earth about anything they ask, it will be done for you by my Father in heaven. For where two or three are gathered in my name, there am I in the midst of them."

Those are the only two places where Jesus uses the word "Church." Of course, Paul and the other New Testament writers use the word a number of times—the word εκκλησια which means "called out," and comes to mean a congregation.

I want to discuss with you these highly controversial words—or have been highly controversial—having to do with the promise of Peter and with the Keys of the Kingdom. And over here where Jesus says "Thou art Peter and on this rock I will build my church." This verse so shakes up Protestants that they try to get around them . . . try to act like they're not there . . . re-interpret them some way, as to say, for example, that Jesus is making a play on words, and that what He really means is that "thou art Peter and on this proclamation that you've made of Me as the Christ I will build My church."

To me, this is an obvious distortion of what Jesus is saying. Jesus is saying, "Peter, I *am* building My church on you, and I am placing great spiritual responsibility upon you," and I think that obviously He *was* giving Peter some promise there. And I think that He *is* saying to Peter that he shall have the responsibility to forgive sins, and to speak of forgiveness, and to speak of sins which are not forgiven.

This doesn't shake me . . . this doesn't disturb me . . . I don't feel like marching to Rome at all. Because nowhere is there any evidence that Peter has any authority or responsibility to pass this on to anybody else, or to become infallible, or to set up a holy see. Jesus is recognizing Peter as a great apostle.

If we take these words with the rigid literalness, let me show you what happens. Here in one verse, Jesus gives Peter this tremendous responsibility . . . and then look what comes immediately thereafter. Remember we were taking these words quite directly that Jesus said to Peter.

Then we read, "From that time (this follows immediately upon the other passage) Jesus began to show his disciples that he must go to Jerusalem and suffer many things from the elders and chief priests and scribes, and be killed, and on the third day be raised. And Peter took Him and began to rebuke Him saying, 'God forbid, Lord! This shall never happen to you.'"

But Jesus turned and said to Peter (Remember he called him a rock just a moment ago) "'Get thee behind me, Satan! You are a hindrance to me; for you're not on the side of God, but of men.'" If He called him a rock several sentences up, He called him Satan now. This is changing your role pretty fast. And if Peter was designed to be infallible, he only remained infallible for about three sentences, because up here he had the power to forgive sins, and down here just below, Jesus says "you are not even speaking for God, you are speaking for men."

When we put things back into their context, and just relax, we realize that if we take Jesus' words as they come along and don't get all disturbed . . . we come out okay.

Let me go over this other passage that I read, where Jesus says to the disciples, "Truly I say to you, whatever you bind on earth shall be bound in heaven, and whatever you loose on earth shall be loosed in heaven." He *is* putting in the hands of the church the responsibility for the forgiveness of sins, I think that's where it belongs, and I shall speak of that in a few moments.

Let me go right on and read this next sentence now, "Again I say to you, if two of you agree on earth about anything they ask, it will be done for them by my Father in heaven."

Now this next that I'm saying, I'm saying with all sincerity. It sounds sacrilegious, but I don't mean it sacrilegiously.

If you're going to take those words about forgiving sin literally, then you have to take these next literally, too.

Yet, I want to bear personal testimony to you, that not two people, but three of us—a mother and father and I—literally prayed all night long that a little girl over in Children's Hospital . . . about two years old with leukemia . . . should not die.

We prayed all night long, and the next morning that little girl died. So here's at least one time when Jesus' promise was not fulfilled.

So of course, there is a real sense in which where Christians get together and pray, God does hear, and God does answer. And there is a real sense in which the Church does have the responsibility for forgiving sins. But for God's sake—and I say it in all reverence—let's keep things in their context.

To study the doctrine of the Church, throughout the whole New Testament, is to find that there are a number of things that have been worked into the life of the Church that should not be there . . . or so it appears to me. For example, most crucially, as I read my whole New Testament, I can find no evidence for a priesthood of any kind.

The very quintessence of Christian theology, it appears to me, is to do away with the role of the priest as one who stands between the people and God except in and as only Christ Himself stands there.

There's one place in First Peter where the Church is spoken of, in toto, as being a holy priesthood.

And so to speak of a branch of the Church that I do dearly love, because I was about halfway reared in it, that is the Episcopal Church, and Dr. Blake's and Dr. Pike's proposal—the fine spirit of which I'm in sympathy with, but to say—both facetiously and seriously—it looks to me that before we can finish working this out, our Episcopal brethren have to get together and rethink the matter of the priesthood so that they can move from their darkness into our marvelous Presbyterian light.

I just don't see any other way to resolve the whole issue.

But to say that I would question the validity of the conception of the minister as being a priest standing between the people and God, once again is not to say that I am not committed to the Church as being the source of the forgiveness of sins, because I am.

In this passage which we read earlier, Jesus clearly gave the Church this power. And I certainly think it's there.

95

But before I say how, let me pause to say that this point about the forgiveness of sins points to a weakness in the typical Protestant American thinking about the Church. You and I, as Americans, are organizers. We organize and join everything. And, therefore, we're inclined to think of the Church as another organization.

Indeed it is not.

The Church is *the Church.* And if a man is a Christian, there's no such thing as his not being a member of the Church. If he's a Christian he's already a member of the Church, and if he's not a Christian, he can't be a member of the Church.

Talk about this thing of being a member. As Americans, we use this word "member" in a way which is completely foreign to the New Testament. To us, a member is a card-holder, a dues payer . . . for example, a member of the Diners' Club.

In the New Testament, the Church is not an organization . . . the Church is an organism, a living body. Therefore, when the New Testament uses the word "member," it uses it in the fine sense that my hand is a member of my living body. And when it speaks of your being a member of the Church, it's in the same sense that my hand is a member of my living body.

So the Church is a body. And the Church, as a body, forgives sins in the only way that sins have ever been forgiven or ever will be forgiven . . . and that is by proclaiming this forgiveness through our Lord Jesus Christ.

The day that the Church ceases offering forgiveness through our Lord Jesus Christ, is the day that forgiveness ceases. And our Lord Jesus was quite aware of this, for having put in the Church the responsibility for proclaiming forgiveness, He then thereby said, "And the Church will never be defeated in this, even to the point of death itself."

I do believe that the Church is catholic, or universal, and I find myself at one with the Roman catholic . . . the Greek catholic . . . the Lutheran catholic . . . the Baptist catholic . . . the Episcopal catholic . . . and Presbyterian catholic . . . all of those together who proclaim our Lord Jesus Christ. And whatever differences there may be, and whatever cleavages I feel—and as some of you know I feel some pretty strong cleavages with some branches of the Church—nevertheless, there is a rock-bottom spot at which I feel myself at one with all of those who share a common love and proclamation of our Lord Jesus Christ.

I believe the Church to be holy.

Now what does the word "holy" mean?
It means worthy of adoration
worthy of veneration
worthy of love
worthy of your respect
and worthy of your sacrifice.

For the Church is the body of Christ.

It is in this frame of reference that I should like to speak of something which I do feel pretty strongly about. And that is this: no one ever has a right to be angry with the Church. You have a right to be angry with ministers . . . I get angry with ministers, get angry with many of them, for ministers are very, very human . . . including this one, who's about 200 per cent human. So you can be angry with ministers . . . you can be angry with members of the church . . . because they all do some pretty stupid and some pretty sub-Christian things. But you can't be angry with the *church*.

As a Christian you have absolutely no right to get angry with the minister, or some fellow member, and go home and pout, and say . . . "Well, I'm not going to have anything to do with the *church* any more."

You have a right to do this: if you find out that any particular church does not serve your spiritual needs, you not only have the right, you have the *responsibility,* to find a church that does.

I'm sure there have been those who, in the history of Westminster, have found out that some how or other Westminster did not meet their needs, and have gone to some other particular church where they could feel a love for our Lord Jesus Christ and serve Him. And this is as it should be.

Then, perhaps, there have been others who have been in some other particular church and found out that they could not love and serve there, and have come to Westminster.

Be that as it is, and is as it should be, but no one has a right to be angry with the Church . . . you're being angry with the body of Christ.

No one has a right to say—nor can any Christian ever say—that he does not need the Church. Of course, he needs the Church. I should like to speak some more about that next week when we're speaking on *the communion of the saints.*

I believe the Church to be the one hope of the world. For the Church is Christ proclaimed and lived in the world.

Whenever I come in in the evening and it's fairly late, I have a practice of watching the Jack Paar show. I'm deeply grateful for the Jack Paar show . . . it serves a marvelous need. That is I can put my mind in neutral when it comes on and can go to sleep at any point I get ready, with the certain assurance that I haven't missed a thing.

The other night Jack Paar had on a clever, witty philosopher . . . a professor from Yale University. Jack Paar does have *this* skill: He's good at asking questions and drawing out those people who are on his program.

This little philosopher was marching along fine untii Jack Paar said to him . . . "Well now, as a philosopher, I'd like to ask you . . . 'What is life all about?' "

And in just a few moments, that little guy was no longer a witty philosopher, but just a pathetic little clown with no makeup on.

For just as soon as you pull Christ out of the focal point of this old world of ours, then those who stand around and cast him aside become pathetic little clowns with no makeup on.

Does Christ's Church make mistakes? God knows that it does, because it's made up of people like you and me. But where the Church is, *Christ* is. And where Christ is, the Church is.

Christ loved His Church, and gave Himself for it.

The apostles tell us that a man should love the Church as he loves his own wife.

And this I shall aspire to do.

March 25, 1962

THE
COMMUNION
OF SAINTS

Y OU AND I HAVE FACED AND WRESTLED with some great things these last few weeks as we have worked through the Apostles' Creed together. We have wrestled with the conception of God the Creator . . . with Christ the Redeemer. We have struggled with the nature of heaven and of the judgment, and some other great and ultimate themes.

We are coming towards the climax in this wrestling through of the Apostles' Creed. We have two great themes yet to face. Next Sunday we shall be dealing with the forgiveness of sins, which lies at the very core of our Christian conception. Thereafter, there will be the Palm Sunday message—sort of a parenthetical Sunday —and then the climax on Easter when we face together those resounding words . . . *I believe in the resurrection of the body and the life everlasting.*

So then to the theme which we confront this Sunday, which by any count would be one of the lesser themes in the Apostles' Creed. There's no question about its truth and its practicality, but perhaps it doesn't drive us back to life's ultimates as do some of the other phrases. But it has its significance.

On each Sunday morning we say, *I believe in the communion of saints*. We shall continue to say it, as we should, and hence it behooves us to know what we mean when we say it.

I believe in the communion of saints.

Let's talk about the phrase some before we face directly its meaning and its implications. As I have said many times in this series, the Apostles' Creed, in its basic form, doubtless had come into existence back in the second century, quite early in the Church's history . . . in its final form, only in the fourth century. But by the beginning of the fourth century, it was in its final form with the exception of two phrases . . . *He descended into hell,* and *I believe in the communion of saints.* It was in the middle of the fourth century that this phrase, *He descended into hell,* first made its appearance in the Apostles' Creed. We talked about it several Sundays ago, and I stated, that for myself, it has so little Biblical basis—and that slim Biblical basis is confusing enough and the phrase is unrewarding enough—that I for one am among those who prefer to leave it out, as do many people in the Presbyterian Church, that is, individual Christians, and many congregations, too.

I don't feel the same way about this phrase that we have today, even though it does not come in until the fifth century. Incidentally, when it was introduced, it immediately surrounded itself with confusion as to its meaning. There is no real certainty as to why it was introduced, or who introduced it, or what was meant by it, when it was originally introduced.

The communion of saints can have—and has been interpreted to have—three basic meanings. It can't be all three; one has to choose between the three. The first is that people in heaven know each other, that that's what *the communion of saints* means. Secondly, there have been those who have said that *the communion of saints* means that people on earth can be in communion with people in heaven. And the third is that *communion of saints* means that church people should get along happily together.

Let us take those up individually.

100

By the time people got around to using this phrase regularly in the Apostles' Creed, it seemed that no one was very much interested in this first interpretation . . . that is that people in heaven know each other. This affirmation seems not to have been particularly emphasized . . . every one seems to have agreed on it. If there is any such thing as heaven, and if Christians go there, presumably they know each other when they get there. So this interpretation never had much popularity.

Up until the time of the Reformation—that is in the 16th century —the Church generally interpreted this phrase to have the second meaning . . . that *the communion of saints* means that I can be in touch with people who are in heaven. This undergirded the Church's teaching about so-called *"saints"* . . . and we shall come back to that word shortly. People to whom people on earth can turn and intercede with for help here on earth . . . that was the most general interpretation of what this phrase meant.

I checked around a little bit and could not find out any late word on how our Roman Catholic brethren interpret this phrase at the moment, but I rather assume that this is still the most popular interpretation within the Roman Catholic communion.

But this third interpretation . . . Calvin and the other reformers said that *the communion of saints* means the fellowship of believers. That is, that church people ought to be good friends with other church people.

This is what it means when I say it. This is what I mean to myself. Obviously it's true. It's not very original, nor is it very earth shaking, but it is important. And before we discuss it, let's clear up the wordage a little bit . . . particularly confusion about this word "saint".

My only reservation about the phrase *the communion of saints* is that the word "saint" has been so distorted as to be almost unsalvageable. Let me say first what it has come to mean, and why, and then what it originally meant.

This is what it has come to mean in mine and your common parlance . . . that a person who is a saint is a sort of a super-good person, one who is really so good as to be kind of super-human. So when we say *that* man is truly a saint, or *that* woman is truly a saint, then they are just about ready to sprout wings and fly. These are the super-people, the hyper-good people.

This interpretation, obviously, comes from the use of the word by our Roman Catholic brethren. That is, that there are people in heaven who were so good on earth that they were able to do what is termed works of supererogation . . . they could do all that was required of them as human beings, and then more, and with this "more" that was done become sort of a storehouse of spiritual good in heaven, which can be dispensed by the Church for the good of those on earth.

And then the doctrine of our Roman Catholic brethren, in line with this . . . that after one dies, these super-good people—with due investigation—can be canonized. That is, they can be officially declared "saints". This is an official title, and once one has been canonized in the Roman Catholic communion, he is therefore, and thereafter, available to the people on earth to be of help in carrying forward life's daily patterns. So, therefore, one turns to St. Christopher and others to be of help with his problems here on earth.

With no desire to be contentious—though doubtless at times I am, but not at the moment—but to set the record straight, let me try to put this phrase back where we can use it. And so let me say that the idea of super-good people is foreign to Scripture.

As a matter of fact, Scripture holds exactly the opposite view. Not only are there not *super-good* people, but according to the New Testament, and according to the Scripture in general . . . there are not even *good* people.

"There's none good . . . no, not one."

All of us fall so far short of what we should be that all of us would rightly come under God's judgment. And therefore, it is God's mercy—his undeserved goodness towards us—that redeems us. We shall be talking about this more at length next week when we talk about *the forgiveness of sins,* but just the opposite of super-good people is there in the Scripture, and this is an unscriptural idea. And in the next place, this use of the word "saint" to refer to a group of super-good people either here on earth or in heaven is completely unscriptural.

102

Here is the Scriptural use of the word. The word "saint" is very common in the Bible, both in the Old Testament and in the New Testament. It may come as a little bit of a surprise to you, that is exactly the same word as "holy." "Kadosh" is the Old Testament Hebrew word.

"Hagios" is the Greek New Testament word.

Both of them are translated the same way. And this same word has already been used twice in the Apostles' Creed, when we refer to *I believe in the Holy Spirit* or *the Holy Ghost,* and in *the holy catholic church.* So we could translate the Creed accurately . . . "I believe in the Holy Ghost, and in the holy catholic church, and in the fellowship of the *holy* people."

When the word "saint" is used in the Old Testament it *always* refers to people on earth. It is usually just the means of referring to God's chosen people, that is, the congregation of Israel.

When we come to the New Testament and the use of the word there, which is crucial for us, we find that once again the word is used rather frequently. And it never refers to a set of super-good people. It is used quite generally and unself-consciously to refer to *all* Christian people, and in such a fashion as to be referring obviously to Christians here on earth.

In the Book of Revelation, and some few other places, the word "saint" does refer to people in heaven, but once again, it means all the Christians who have died, and not some special category.

So the word "saint" means simply and undramatically "a Christian." Hence, however much it may shock you, and surprise you, and upset you

I am a saint

Charlie Owens is a saint

Gene Grier is a saint

Dana Brown is a saint

and each one of you is a saint.

So will you please refer to me hereafter as St. Cliff.

And I shall reciprocate in my reference to you.

So we're all saints. We have no more worries. And in reality this is right, because as saints, we are God's select people.

I'm coming back to that in just a moment.

The word "communion"—*the communion of the saints*—this is the Latin word "communionem," which just means "fellowship." Back of this is the idea of having or holding in common. And hence the word, this *communion of saints,* is etymologically, the same word as "communism." If you were going to translate "communism" into Greek you would use the word "κοινωνια." It would be a little shocking once again, but there would be a certain propriety in speaking of the "communism of the saints."

Out of all this there is a central significant conviction, preserved by this phrase, and very important, and *quite* Scriptural. And that is this . . . that we Christians should have a special love for each other.

One of the earliest and most deeply moving traditions of the Church, is that back in the days of the persecution—when the pagan world first started taking note of the fact that there was such a thing as the Christian Church—one of the things that was most characteristically applied to them, was the pagans would say "See how these Christians love each other."

I've preached on this idea before, not so long ago, and hence the things that I say from here on to the end may sound just a little bit repetitious, but they need to be said in this setting.

There is a real sense in which we Christians should have a special love for each other. This feeling for each other should be built on the conviction regarding the way God feels about us as Christians.

There is a popular phrase used in and out of the Church that is quite religious sounding . . . *the fatherhood of God and the brotherhood of man.* There is a sense in which this is quite true, and needs to be repeated, but there is a sense in which it is misleading. *The fatherhood of God* means that God is the Creator of all men, and yearns to be acknowledged as the Heavenly Father of all men. And *the brotherhood of man* means that the human race is one, and that men should be brothers. So, really, *the fatherhood*

104

of God and *the brotherhood of man* voices not the way things are in this old world of ours.

Obviously, God is not the Heavenly Father of all men, for a large part of the world will not claim Him at all, or claim Him only in some distorted sense. And obviously, there is not brotherhood in the world. This is an aspiration, not a reality of the moment . . . not how things are, but how they should be. In talking about *the fatherhood of God* and *the brotherhood of man,* we are very likely to confuse ourselves.

The whole conception of saints, that *is* Scriptural is that the saints are a holy people, λαος αγιος. They're holy not in the sense of being super-good, but holy in the sense of being set-off and being God's special people. Hence, it must be said, that there is a real sense in which our Heavenly Father has a relationship with His saints—us—that He cannot have with the rest of humanity.

If one wants to see this under-girded in Scripture, he turns to one of the most moving passages in the Bible, and that is John, the 17th chapter, where our Lord Jesus at the culmination of His ministry is making His great high priestly prayer in behalf of His Church.

In this prayer He speaks of Himself first as having come to redeem the world, and then right after that He says "And now, Heavenly Father, I pray not for the world but for these whom thou has given me."

In other words, He takes those who are claiming Him as Lord and Master of Life, and says, "Now Heavenly Father, there is a prayer which I want to make especially for these folk who have come to claim Thee as Heavenly Father through Me." And so our Lord Jesus proceeds to pray especially for those who are His.

Someone could take this and push it to the point where it once again becomes a distortion of the truth. But there is a truth here which you and I need to hold on to. We can make a rough analogy within our own human lives. The reason that God has a special relationship with His saints is because His saints have a special relationship with Him.

How many of you parents have said to me, either in the intimacy of my study or in some conversation which you and I were having, in which we were talking about our children, and in which our children were not there, and you and I might voice a feeling that we might not voice otherwise . . . how many of you have said to me, "Well now, here's this child, or this child, or this child that you're talking about with certain characteristics, and then you would mention this child, and say, "Now this is the one who loves everybody . . . this is the one who is so affectionate and so outgoing that I just can't help but have a special love for him."

You can't help but love him, because he loves everybody else so much.

There's a sense in which God Almighty can pour out His love on us as He cannot on the rest of the world, because of our having found a way to love Him through our Lord, Jesus Christ. *And,* the awareness of this relationship with God, brings us back to *the communion of the saints.* Because we have a special relationship with God, it means that we can and should have a special relationship with each other.

Knowing about God's love for men in my heart does a little something for my life. Not as much as it should, but a little bit.

This enables me to know something about what God's love for you does in *your* heart. Not as much as it should do, but a little bit.

Knowing about this love of God for us means that I can trust you just a little bit more than I can trust the rest of the world. And you can trust me just a little bit more.

It means that I can forgive you just a little bit more readily for hurts, real and imagined. And that you can forgive me a little bit more readily for hurts, real and imagined.

There is a sense, then, in which I can serve you more sacrificially than I can serve the rest of the world, and in which you can serve me more sacrifically than you can serve the rest of the world.

So there *is* such a thing as *the communion of saints*—the feeling of a closeness together—because we can have a little bit more trust

a little bit more love
　　a little bit more sacrifice
　　　　a little bit more forgiveness for each other
than we dare offer the rest of the world . . . a sense in which
we stand closer together as we face the world.

I think this really happens.

And so on Sunday morning, when I say *I believe in the communion
of saints* I believe *this* takes place in *this* church *all* the time.

Perhaps not as it should
　　but it's real
　　　　and it's rich
　　　　　　and it's Christian.

April 1, 1962

THE
FORGIVENESS
OF SINS

"SINCE WE ARE JUSTIFIED BY FAITH," says the great Apostle, "we have peace with God through our Lord Jesus Christ. Through Him we have obtained access to this grace in which we stand, and we rejoice in our hope of sharing the glory of God. More than that, we rejoice in our sufferings, knowing that suffering produces endurance, and endurance produces character, and character produces hope, and hope does not disappoint us because God's love has been poured into our hearts through the Holy Spirit which has been given to us.

"While we were yet helpless, at the right time Christ died for the ungodly. While one would hardly die for a righteous man, though perhaps for a good man one would dare even to die. But God shows His love for us in that while we were yet sinners, Christ died for us."

Time and further experience are proving that there were a number of places where the great psychologist, Sigmund Freud, was wrong about human personality. But time and experience are giving growing and overwhelming evidence to that which vaguely we already knew . . . that he was terrifyingly right in many places . . . and nowhere more right and nowhere more terrifyingly right than in his contention concerning the depth and the breadth of human guilt . . . seeing in this malady the malignancy out of which so much of the ills of mankind extend.

Freud's analysis of guilt had been long recognized and reported by Scripture, but men had many times insisted on misreading Scripture. Of course, Freud had to talk about guilt because he could not talk about sin. He could not talk about sin because he did not believe in it. But as far as Scripture is concerned— and as far as you and I are concerned—guilt and sin are the two sides of the same coin . . . for our guilt is the feeling we have about our sin.

Life can be miserable enough, God knows, but it would be truly unbearable and has many times demonstrated itself to be unbearable if and where man does not have the privilege and the power to stand and say, as you and I say each Sunday morning, *I believe in the forgiveness of sins.*

In proclaiming those mighty words in the Creed, we come towards the culmination of the Creed. And those words, *I believe in the forgiveness of sins,* should be right at the culmination, just this side of those final magnificent words which we shall proclaim two weeks from today when we announce to the world, *I believe in the resurrection of the body and the life everlasting.*

This morning we shall come back to the matter of guilt, but for the time being, I should like for us to stick with the matter of sin and forgiveness.

Let's talk about sin first.

What is sin? Well, our Presbyterian Shorter Catechism defines sin this way . . . "Sin is any want of conformity unto, or transgression of, the law of God." The Catechism says sin is breaking the law. And I should like to dare this morning to take issue with the Catechism and to say that I believe that this is one of the places where the Catechism—whereas it is being Scriptural— could be much more profoundly Scriptural if it took a deeper— and what I think is a much more basic attitude—toward what sin really is.

When we turn to the writer of the Book of Genesis . . . when we turn to the Old Testament prophets . . . when we turn to our

Lord Jesus himself, or to the Apostle Paul . . . we get this more profound interpretation of sin.

What is it? Sin is selfish rebellion.

Always the story of Adam and Eve remains as the classic description of what sin really is. Let me remind you of several things about this great story. The whole story is designed to show that sin is not an act—hear me—sin is not an act, but an attitude . . . not what one does, *but the way one feels.*

And this story is deliberately, and profoundly, built around one little incidental, inconsequential act. Here is a fruit tree and someone goes and pulls one piece of fruit from the tree and partakes of it and thereby changes the whole destiny of mankind . . . this one, deliberate, superficial act. How could we ever do anything but recognize that the whole implication of this approach was to thrust us past this little superficial act to the meaning of the act itself.

Listen to this crucial verse. The serpent is talking and he says, "God knows that in the day that you eat thereof (he's talking to Eve) you shall be as God, knowing good and evil."

Let me paraphrase this for you because this is what the serpent is saying, "You shall be your *own* God, determining for yourself good and evil."

There it is.

Sin is putting self in the center of life, rather than God.

Sin is making self one's own God.

How can I emphasize this? The story of Adam and Eve is not designed to show where sin came from. It's designed, rather, to show *what sin is*—not the source, but the nature—for every man, of course, is his own Adam and every woman is her own Eve. Each one of us, like Eve, takes that which is inherently good and seizes it and shakes it in the face of God to say, "This is my declaration of independence."

There is a great difference between breaking the law and being in rebellion. In the relationship with our nation, we readily make

110

this distinction. If a citizen breaks a federal law—as many citizens do each day—no one considers this inconsequential. Everyone recognizes that such laws being broken calls for a penalty to be paid.

But for a man to be in *rebellion* against his nation . . . you and I have quite a different feeling about that. We have a different vocabulary, as we should. About such a man, we use the ugly word, "traitor," or "insurrectionist" or "seditionist."

You and I feel quite differently—and properly so—about a man who breaks a multitude of laws, but is at long last loyal to his nation, as over against a man who may keep *all* of the laws and is basically disloyal to his nation.

One is a lawbreaker, but the other is a *traitor*.

Sin is ultimate disloyalty to God . . . not just breaking several laws. This disloyalty to God consists in making one's self his own ultimate source of loyalty. And all of us are guilty of that . . . each one of you . . . and I.

I should like to offer you a little analogy here—something that you can check for yourself in your own life—and that is what happened in your growing from childhood into adulthood in relationship with your own parents. When you were a little child, you rebelled many times against the law, and the rules, and the regulations, and the restrictions, but not particularly against the person.

Whereas, in that strange period of adolescence where you properly have to get to the place where you reject your parents as your superiors in order to reaccept them as your equal . . . here there comes rebellion, and the rebellion manifests itself in the breaking of the law. One breaks the law in order to manifest the rebellion.

To show you what happens to little children, let me pull almost at random one of our family stories. We all have a multitude of them, but I happen to recall something that happened when my brother, Ashby, was a small youngster . . . I don't know, four or five years old, maybe a little younger.

He loved to go in the kitchen and turn on all of the gas burners. Maybe he liked the smell of gas, I don't know, but anyhow he'd go in and turn on the gas burners, which, of course, was not designed to be a particularly safe practice, and my Aunt urged him over and over not to do it . . . to no avail.

One day they were standing in the living room, looking out of the bay window, and across the street there was a man whom we knew in the neighborhood, who had suffered painfully and tragically from arthritis . . . to such an extent that he walked with his back almost at a 90 degree angle, almost parallel to the ground, so he leaned over, had to keep his arm behind his back and hold his head way up and walked in this terrible position to try to maintain his balance and reduce the pain until this had been hardened into the position in which he had to walk. Auntie, out of her desperation, saw this man walking across the street and she pointed him out to Ashby and said, "See that man. Now the reason he has to walk that way is because when he was a little boy he kept turning on the gas."

I'll let you guess what happened.

About five minutes later, Ashby walks out, bent way over with his hand behind his back and Auntie goes in the kitchen and turns off the gas.

You see, it was impossible for Ashby to resist this marvelous fascination of walking around in such an appealing fashion which could be brought about by such a simple device as turning on the gas. And rebellion against Auntie was the least of his concerns.

But there comes a point when the breaking of the law is for the sake of the rebellion. And that which is necessary, and right, and inevitable, and let us even say proper within man in his relationship with man becomes the quintessence of tragedy in his relationship with God.

I should like to say this thing in such a way that you could not possibly forget it, and I don't know how to do it. What I'm saying is *crucial* to the understanding of what Christianity is all about, and the only thing I know how to do is just to repeat it a couple of times and maybe it will stick.

Sin is attitude towards God, rather than acts against God. The acts are incidental.

112

Let me repeat it.

Sin is attitude towards God, rather than acts against God. The acts are incidental.

We prefer to reduce life to acts . . . to deeds. When we do, we make the futile superficial mistake over and over again of dividing life into black and white, right and wrong.

Here are all the good deeds and here are all the bad deeds, and a deed is either good or evil. In reality—whereas there is good and evil—God knows when he's the source of the distinction. Nevertheless, our acts are on a spectrum which goes all the way from the white over to the black in an unbroken line of increasing intensity, with most of our acts being here in the gray area . . . mixtures of good and evil . . . this being inevitable because in the first place, our motives are so bady mixed. In any given act there is some good motivation and some evil motivation. Beyond that, our knowledge is extremely limited, and almost any act that we perform has limited goodness in it and limited evil. The outcome is always a mixture of good and evil.

I'm fairly well convinced that—by the mercy of God—we are precluded from ever doing that which is completely evil. By our own sinfulness and selfness, we are prevented from doing that which is ever completely good. Our acts lie somewhere here in the middle.

I'm convinced that seldom, if ever, do we perform an act which represents pure gain in terms of what we would aspire to have accomplished. By the grace of God we are forbidden—or rather prevented, I think—from ever performing an act which represents complete loss.

This has to do, in my own mind, with our convictions regarding the nature of man.

Let me take a moment just to make comparisons.

I think that we are talking about an area which our Presbyterianism —our Calvinism, if you please—drives us closer to the New Testament and to the Scripture than any other approach within

Christendom that I know. I say that with sincerity, not with pride. As in contrast, this is said not in condemnation, but to try to make a contrast which I think is valid.

Our Methodist brethren and our Roman Catholic brethren are much more inclined to take a superficial view of sin.

For example, official Roman Catholic theology says that when man falls he loses all of his super qualities, but he still is able to live a perfect life and even to pile up works of supererogation.

Our Methodist brethren feel that when a man makes his profession of faith he moves into a state of grace, that is, where he is not sinning and presumably could stay there. Of course, he does sin and has to come back and be saved again. This distinction is more in the minds of the theologians than it is in the minds of the laymen, but it's there.

We Presbyterians take a much more serious view of sin.

We say that sin drives right on down to the heart of man and that man is essentially evil. We take a right grim view of mankind. Therefore, it has been said that Presbyterianism, as you know, never keeps anybody from sinning . . . it just keeps him from getting any fun out of it . . . and this may be.

All right. This is as over against the attitude which you find in your sociology books and in social sciences, which says that man is essentially good and ignorant. If we can just educate him . . . then the goodness comes out and he'll be all right.

Presbyterians say he is both *evil* and ignorant . . . it's all right to educate him, but it's not going to get rid of the evil that's down inside because he's going to remain in rebellion.

I think time is proving us Presbyterians right.

Go home and think this over. Keep clearly in mind that when we think about God's forgiving us, it means not just forgiving our acts. I don't think He has much trouble with that—though our acts can be pretty vicious and pretty ruthless—but over against what He *really* has to forgive, I think that forgiving our acts comes fairly easily.

114

Take note of this: You're on a crowded bus and you are, as you should be, facing towards the front, you're holding on to a strap, or a rail—or whatever you hold onto to keep from being pushed over—and here you are looking down the street and minding your own business, and all of a sudden the man behind you gives you such a tremendous shove with his shoulder as to almost knock you down. Instantly you feel this surge of anger. And with the flush of anger on your face, you turn around to make some ugly comment, only to have him say, "Gee, I'm sorry." Then you look and you see that behind him there's a man who in this closely crowded bus has been overcome and has fainted, and so this guy says, "The fellow back of me fainted and fell against me—I'm so sorry."

Instantly your feelings change . . . you forget about what has happened . . . and both of you turn around to help the chap who has fallen down here on the floor.

The act remains exactly the same, your feelings changed instantly when you were aware of the difference in attitude.

For God to forgive us means that you and I go down through life and over and over again we thrust our shoulders against God as hard as we can, and when He turns around to see what happened, we're not even looking—we're acting as though He were not even there—and God Almighty forgives *that*.

So it is in that frame of reference that we come to talk about Christian sermons by fine Christian ministers, who have pointed out with validity and with Christian insight the attitude of the people . . . the fickleness of the crowd . . . the jealousy of the Pharisees.

Then at the culmination of his sermon, that minister has legitimately turned to you and has said, "Were you there when they crucified my Lord?" And you've had to say, "Yes, I was, because my attitude is the same as that."

What's God's attitude?

Jesus said, "He that hath seen me hath seen the Father." Then Jesus said, "Father, forgive them, for they know not what they do."

That's the reason that you and I have to pray over, and over, and over again for God's forgiveness. He has to forgive us all these acts, to be sure, but the devastating thing is that he has to forgive our attitude, which never really does anything better than improve just a little bit.

In closing, let's go back to guilt. That's the reason that you get down on your knees and pray, "Dear God, forgive this, and this, and this, and this" . . . and get up still with the guilt down inside, because you really don't want to give it up. That's the reason that you and I keep interpreting sin as the breaking of the laws because that makes God impersonal.

I can break this law, and this law, and this law. I might decide to change my mind and keep these laws and still I wouldn't have to deal with God Almighty. Breaking the law is impersonal, so it's nice to be able to say that when I sin, I break the law.

It's devastating to say that sin is rebellion, for that breaks the heart of God.

Sin as rebellion is serious. It's hard for God to forgive that, I guess, but He does . . . He does.

April 8, 1962

THE
RESURRECTION
OF THE BODY

THE FACT THAT THERE ARE so many of us here today means
either that something *has* happened that is pretty important
    that something *is* happening
        or that something is *going* to happen quite important.

I am convinced that it is all three
    that something important *has* happened
      is happening
        and is *going* to happen
and therefore, it is very right and proper that we should all be here.

That makes it time for my little annual Easter speech which I
have made on previous Easters and will make on coming Easters.
That is to say that each one of you—every one of you—is most
cordially welcomed at this Easter service.

I have no patience at all with cynicism regarding Easter day.
I'm real pleased that there is a tremendous crowd.

And I hope every Christian church in the country is just spilling
over. I do not think you came to church to show off your clothes;
I think you came to worship God Almighty, and to celebrate
the resurrection of His Christ.

If there are any of you who by any happenstance have not been to this church previously, we are most delighted to have you today. If there's any one of you who hasn't been here in a long time, I can't think of any better day to come back to church, than on the day on which we celebrate the resurrection of our Lord, Jesus Christ.

And if by any turn of events it should come about that between now and next Easter, for any reason, personal or circumstantial, you should find yourself facing another Easter without having attended church in the meantime—I hope this will not be, but should it be—I want you to know this is one church where you will be most cordially welcomed. If we need to, we'll put chairs around the front and up here on the rostrum, and get Charlie to move over.

So we are delighted to have you on Easter Day.

Since there may be some of you who are here for the first time or who haven't been here in some time, let me say that I should like to treat you like a member of the family—which indeed you are—and catch you up on the fact that the rest of us have been working away, since just after Christmas, on a series of sermons on the Apostles' Creed . . . this universal creed of Christendom, the oldest of the creeds established, probably, and gotten together sometime, perhaps, in the second century.

On this Easter day, all of the Christian Church will be proclaiming this Creed together. Sunday after Sunday we have been working through phrase after phrase, having timed the series in such a way that here on Easter Sunday we can come to the last great, culminating phrase . . .

I believe in the resurrection of the body and the life everlasting.

The resurrection of the body and the life everlasting.

Now in order to sharpen our focus on our subject for today, let me say that we have here two phrases, so related that if either one is true, the other is true. And so we can compress them into one, and then having compressed them, take the more difficult —and hence the more challenging of the two—for our center of focus.

118

Let us recognize that if we believe in the resurrection in any realistic fashion at all, then we believe, as an outgrowth of that, in the life everlasting.

For the sake of clarity, let me repeat something that I have said several times in this series on the Creed:

that this word translated here *"everlasting"* is really the Greek word αιωνιος which means—as is clearly manifested a number of places in the New Testament—not *"ever lasting"*, but *eternal"*. And the word *"eternal"* means not *"endless time"* but
  "not bound by time"
  "an absence of time".

So when we think of life everlasting, we should say *"eternal life"*, a life into which we move not bound by space or time. The fact that we cannot conceive it, makes it in no less sense, a reality.

So to say, I believe in the resurrection of the body and the life eternal, and to focus then back again upon the resurrection of the body.

What does that mean?

Well, it could mean some things that are right ridiculous . . . which it doesn't mean, and I don't think ever did mean.

I should like to clarify a couple of the things that I think *the resurrection of the body* does not mean. I do not think it means that there will come a day of universal physical resuscitation when everybody gets back into the same flesh and blood he was in at some previous time.

To dispose of this idea, I must momentarily make something of a rather morbid comment. I do it only in order to try and clarify the situation.

In the course of human history, there has been an elaborate overlapping of the use of the stuff out of which physical bodies are made. To push this morbid comment only one step further . . . in man's conflict with man, so many times there have been the battlefields, covered with human flesh, bodies having been buried just beneath the surface to become in time, that which enriched the very crops that were grown thereon. And to see therein, how it becomes a cyclical matter to make ridiculous and unrealistic the idea of there ever being the resuscitation of each person's flesh. We wouldn't quite be sure who would get what. So that's one thing that *the resurrection of the body* does not mean.

While I'm involved in this verbal bulldozing of what I consider some of the mental debris which surrounds this great doctrine, I should like to continue.

I'd like to say several other things that I think *the resurrection of the body* does not mean. Here I shall be taking issue—not critically, but directly and sincerely and deeply—with a number of Easter sermons which I have heard and read . . . sermons which you have heard and read . . . perhaps of such kinds as will be preached today.

Therefore, I must say that I do not believe that *the resurrection of the body* is a nice, quaint, old-fashioned way of saying "I believe in the immortality of the human soul."

I shall set out here to take a little bit more direct issue with those who would so contend, and will be taking some issue with some good preaching by some good preachers . . . Christian men. I may be using more courage than wisdom. I'm not asking you to agree with everything that I say . . . I'm only asking you to listen and to make up your own mind.

I'm saying to you that there are many fine sermons, by many fine preachers, that go something like this—though I have to take issue with them—they begin this way . . . "To say that one believes in the resurrection of the body means that one recognizes that every man has an immortal soul." The sermon then proceeds to offer presumable proof, and the proof runs along like this . . . "First, God is immortal, and there is something of God in every man, therefore, there is something in every man that cannot die." Then the argument moves along further and says, somewhat plaintively, I think . . . "We cannot believe that God will ultimately destroy anything which He has created." Then the sermon moves on, and will move on joyously—we must recognize on a day like this—to the glorious and thrilling renewal of life which each Spring brings, and with the presumption that that thereby proves immortality.

120

Then it moves on towards the culmination, does such a sermon, by saying that as one looks around on mankind—from the most primitive to the most advanced—one finds this universal yearning for immortality. It is to be presumed that if God Almighty put this yearning in the heart of man, then it must mean that the immortality is there.

It may be that some of these arguments I have overlooked, but it would be no matter because, as I have indicated, I would reject them along with these others.

My feelings get involved here, because my anger somewhat wells up at the way that our Lord Jesus Christ and His Resurrection get treated in such an approach.

It would appear to me that when the preacher, however sincerely, gets down to the end of all the arguments that he can think of for the immortality of the soul, then he drags in Christ and His resurrection as sort of a clincher to stop all arguments. It appears that if all of the arguments have been good up until now, the resurrection is just about as superfluous as anything can get.

Rather than to say in some pedantic fashion, step by step, why I reject each one of these other arguments as being specious, or groundless, or fruitless, let me say rather that I believe that *the resurrection of the body* as a doctrine
    properly begins with the resurrection of Christ
      continues with the resurrection of Christ
        stops with the resurrection of Christ.

This is exactly what the Church has always preached at its best, right from Pentecost on. And this is all that the Bible knows. Paul, John, James, the writer of the Book of Hebrews . . . all the other New Testament writers . . . read them as much as you like. You find no talk about flowers in the Spring, you find no talk of every man being a part of God, you find no talk of man's invincible surmise. You find these men saying simply, directly, and unequivocably "Christ rose from the dead." This means that if you claim Him as Lord, God will raise you from the dead, too. Then there comes a glorious "Halleluja". Say these men in the New Testament, take it or leave it, there it is. They considered that this was such a glorious reality, that it was worth going around the world to proclaim. If man would believe it, it would turn the world upside down.

When these folks in the New Testament spoke of the resurrection they knew pretty concretely what they meant. They meant an empty tomb. They meant a recognizable Jesus in a garden on a Sunday morning. And note this, because it's fairly crucial, that this resurrected Christ was both recognizable and unrecognizable . . . at times recognized, at times not recognized . . . both changed and the same. And I should like to come back to that passingly for a moment just a bit later.

After we have wandered around through all of the vapid speculations about this thing of immortality of the soul, to me it's wonderful to come back to this book, the Bible, which is so refreshingly realistic. You can accept it, or reject it, but it speaks its piece. As I have said, the Bible knows nothing of a beautiful, wispy little soul, which like the butterfly, finally breaks out from its nasty old body and goes floating off into heaven.

The Bible knows nothing of such a soul at all, in that sense, for the Bible—when it speaks of man—knows man only as body and spirit, one indissoluble whole, bound indestructively into one. You cannot talk of the body without the spirit, or the spirit without the body.

So whatever you want to do with man in this world, or any world to come, you must do it to him as an entity, says the Bible. This is a nice, healthy, realistic view of man, and when firmly held to, does away with more vain, sub-Christian, foolish thinking than almost any doctrine I know.

For example, to get man firmly bound into this body and spirit unity, so that it is not broken apart, does away with all of this vain Eastern speculation about some independent little soul that ends up in reincarnations over and over again. To get man tightly bound together into this Biblical unity, does away with this sort of moral dualism wherein one thinks of the flesh as doing bad things, but my pure little soul down inside is not touched by the flesh, and therefore I do pretty much as I please. The Bible puts it on the lines that man is this great unity, to believe in or disbelieve, but keep it realistic.

So then somebody will say, "Well now, what of this point that you made at the beginning about the flesh . . . and there are some things that *the resurrection of the body* did not mean . . . and these comments that you're making about the things that were a little bit grim?"

The Apostle Paul had this same question asked of him by the Corinthian Christians. I think that Paul felt that they were being a little bit "tongue in cheek" when they asked how the body could be resurrected, because Paul was a little bit petulant in his answer at the beginning.

This reminds me of a not very gracious phrase that we used to say when we were in college when we thought we were pretty smart. We'd go around saying, "I don't mind ignorance, but I hate stupidity."

The Apostle Paul was saying to his fellow Christians there in Corinth, "I don't mind ignorance, but I hate stupidity." He went on to say that when you're talking about the resurrection of the body, you should not be like children in your thinking. He raises the question, "How will the dead be raised up . . . with what kind of body do they come?"

Then he goes on to give an analogy.

"What you sow does not come to life unless it dies. What you sow is not the body which is to be, but a bare kernel, perhaps of wheat or of some other grain. But God gives it a body as he has chosen, and to each kind of seed, its own body. Men, and animals, and birds each have their own kind of flesh. There is one glory of the sun, another glory of the moon, and another glory of the stars, for stars differ from stars in glory. So," says he, "there is a resurrection body, but not a fleshy body. Let's not get into this kind of foolishness."

This is why I like this presentation of the New Testament where our Lord Jesus in between this time of His crucifixion and His resurrection leaves as an enigma as to where He is and what becomes of Him. I'm grateful that these different stories of the resurrection leave us with some conflict as to the manner and method of His appearance when He came back, lest we get too dogmatic in the form and the nature of the resurrection body. Here it is . . . our basic Christian assurance that everything about you that is important is destined to conquer death.

Accept it or reject it, but there it is. That makes everything about you, and this life, and this world, and our conduct, and our meanings, and our values . . . it makes all those things important. Which is just as it should be.

Easter offers not some little flowery hope for this wispy little soul that shall float off into a wispier heaven. But the bodily resurrection means that *all of you*—if it is of any consequence except that filled tooth, and that broken leg, and that bald head . . . and I think God Almighty can safely assume that we don't want to bother with those anyway (at least, I'm glad for him to so safely assume in my own instance) but aside from that aspect of the thing —everything about you and me that is important, moves through this sphere in which we live into eternal life.

Do you and I actually believe in Christ's resurrection?

As you sit in this church this morning do you really believe that Christ rose from the dead?

I think sometimes you do. I think sometimes I do, and sometimes our fellow Christians do. When we do, our lives take on such a glow of assurance and warmth that the world finds us and our Christ irresistible.

Sometimes we only half believe, and sometimes we don't believe at all. Why?

I've tried to determine—and all I can report to you is what I have found from searching my own heart—and you shall have to search your own heart and come to your own conclusion.

But I suspect as I look at my own soul that the reason why my belief in the resurrected Christ gets awfully fuzzy and weak at times is because if there really *is* a resurrected Christ there doesn't seem to be much room left in my heart for a selfish, unresurrected life.

I believe in the resurrection of the body—both Christ's and mine.

124

When I believe that, it means that I am the kind of person who knows that I shall go right on living to my richest fullness in this life, and that at the end of this temporal life, take everything of me that is worth carrying along, and move without missing a pace right on through this dark mystery called death.

That's right glowing and rewarding living.

The idea of Easter is to get us away from this sort of selfishness that keeps invading our souls from time to time, and push selfishness off of the throne long enough for a really risen, resurrected, living Christ to move back into the center of life.

And, then, that makes every Sunday an Easter
    it makes every morning an Easter
        it makes every moment an Easter.

And believe me, that's living!

April 22, 1962